Beasts of the Forest:
Denizens of the Dark Woods

T0385685

Beasts of the Forest:
Denizens of the Dark Woods

Edited by Jon Hackett and Seán Harrington

British Library Cataloguing in Publication Data

Beasts of the Forest: Denizens of the Dark Woods

A catalogue entry for this book is available from the British Library

ISBN: 0 86196 740 7 (Paperback))
ISBN: 0 86196 957 9 (ebook-MOBI)
ISBN: 0 86196 958 6 (ebook-EPUB)
ISBN: 0 86196 959 3 (ebook-EPDF)

Published by
John Libbey Publishing Ltd, 205 Crescent Road, East Barnet, Herts EN4 8SB,
United Kingdom
e-mail: john.libbey@orange.fr; web site: www.johnlibbey.com

Distributed worldwide by **Indiana University Press**,
Herman B Wells Library – 350, 1320 E. 10th St., Bloomington, IN 47405, USA.
www.iupress.indiana.edu

Printed and bound in the United States of America.

Contents

From the Beasts of the Forest conference at St Mary's University, Twickenham, 1 July 2017.
Image courtesy of Valerian Entertainment.

Acknowledgements

We would like to take this opportunity to thank all of the speakers that have contributed to our conference series, which has to date covered *Beasts of the Deep*, *Beasts of the Forest* and finally *Beasts of the Sky*. Over the course of three symposia between 2016 and 2018, we were privileged to hear over 50 speakers present papers. We thank each of these presenters for volunteering their time, expertise and creativity.

These conferences would not have been possible were it not for the organisational expertise of Suzanne Gilbert, to whom we are eternally indebted!

We would like to thank our wonderfully talented illustrator Rupert Norfolk, for providing his abundant talents in creating memorable images across each of these collections. Our colleague Lee Brooks has kindly contributed the striking cover to this volume.

Finally we would like to offer a dedication to the memory of Peter Hutchings, who provided the wonderful keynote presentation for *Beasts of the Forest* in 2017. We were greatly saddened to hear of Peter's passing, and thank him for his memorable contribution.

Belebte Waldstraße (1605) – Brueghel the Elder

Introduction

Beasts of the Forest

I n the painting *Belebte Waldstraße* (1605) – Jan Brueghel the Elder captures a small but significant moment from everyday life in the early 17th century. We see a medieval highway, leading into a dense and dark forest. The overhanging trees shadow the earthen road, and along this road we see travellers, merchants and horsemen, coming and going. These paths into the dense forests of central Europe were significant routes that joined people, cities and farmland. They were the veins that would later carry the life-force of the enlightenment – shining light into the dark ages and washing away our fears of the natural worlds. In medieval times, the forest could be a threatening place – home to dangerous animals alongside myths and legends.

In present times, the Western world can seem like a monstrous place. Socio-political strife and cultural upheaval seem intertwined with impending ecological disaster. The administration of Donald Trump and his intermediaries have continually downplayed the existence of climate change, and have been active in the removal of federal protections to the environment within the United States and beyond (*The Guardian*, 2017). Jair Bolsonaro, president of Brazil and named by some 'Trump of the Tropics', has committed to dialling back his country's protections for the Amazon rainforest and has suggested pulling Brazil out of the 1993 Paris agreement (Nature, 2018). Here in Europe, our last remaining tract of primeval forest – Białowieża forest in Poland – was up until recently being threatened by renewed logging, which saw some 200,000 cubic meters of ancient trees cut down (Cole, 2018). The forest would have continued to be reduced, were it not for timely action by the European Court of Justice (Żmihorski *et al*, 2018).

In early 2019, at the World Economic Forum in Davos, Sir David Attenborough pleaded and begged world leaders at the very least to acknowledge the threat posed to the natural world: 'We can wreck it with ease, we can wreck it without even noticing.' (BBC, 2019) The dulcet tones of his famous voice, continually imploring us not to forget that the ecological disasters of land and sea implicate us all, and it is up to us to take action before it is too late. Though what specific actions can be taken against the growing tide of human expansion and industrialisation, Attenborough does not specify.

When did the natural world cease to be threatening and when did it start to become so acutely threatened? This is a question to hold, during the course of the following collection. The papers enclosed within this text, offer a variety of analyses of threatening apparitions of the forest – the media texts that represent arboreal contexts as monstrous in themselves, or as home to monsters. It is hoped that by initiating these discussions, we can ascertain the cultural attraction and appeal of these 'threatening' forest apparitions – as images of what is essentially one of the most threatened ecological contexts in the 21st century.

Conjuring the spirits of the Frankfurt School (or alternatively Althusser, (1971)), popular media texts can offer us a look into the ideologies of the industries and culture within which we exist. The western 'Culture Industry', as described by Adorno and Horkheimer (1944), is still animated by the spirit of the industrial revolution – the ideals of enlightenment and modernism that sought to push back the boundaries of the wild, the superstitious and the esoteric – enabling plenty and minimising want.

Yet despite the socio-cultural movements that sought to expel and repress our fear of our natural world, these spaces and places come back to haunt our popular imagination – reworked and mediated by commercial apparatuses – that produce, distribute and exhibit our popular media.

Over the last 10 years, the academic field of 'monstrosity' has gained renewed interest, as evidenced in several collections – Asma (2009), Wright (2013) and indeed our precursor to this text: *Beast of the Deep: Sea Creatures and Popular* Culture (2018). Among recent discussions – James Eli Adams (2018) questions the scientific discourses around 'monstrosity' – that position the monstrous as 'anomalies that instilled "radical fear" ' (Adams, 2018, p. 776). Radical, perhaps, in its ability to conjure up a sense that the world around us is changing, and at times we can feel powerless to affect these changes. Perhaps we have become so complacent in the natural world's vulnerability and impending destruction that fantasies of this space as 'threatening' once again hold a strange appeal.

Continually in our popular media, we see the forest designated as a 'threatening' space, filled with horrors of human or supernatural creation. Indeed, a wave of Scandi-noir-inspired television series begin with or contain a young woman, being chased through the woods by a killer – starting with the Danish production *Forbrydelsen* (2007). This was repeated and repacked across national boundaries – France: *La Forêt* (2017), Germany: *Dark* (2017) and the United States: *The Killing* (2011–2014). The forest is such a common horror geography, that one does not have to go far to find threatening arboreal spaces. Recent films such as *The Ritual* (2017), *The Witch* (2015) and *Apostle* (2018), all position the forest as a point and place of archaic connection with primordial and esoteric horrors.

Yet these tendencies can be followed into the recent and far past – the expressed fears of settling Puritans in North America positioned the forests as the direct opponent of their work in 'civilising' their new landscape (Ringel, 2017). Their anxieties over whether they had discovered a new-Eden, or hell on earth, were played out in their folk-tales and anxieties as projected on to these dark and foreboding woods, a tendency repeatedly expressed in the literature and storytelling practices of North America up to recent times – from the dark woods of American Gothic literature, to the haunted woods of contemporary American television (from *Twin Peaks* (1990–1991) and *The X-Files* (1993–2002) to *Grimm* (2011–) and *Sabrina* (2018–), among many others).

This collection forms a series of discussions of these beasts of the woods, as they appear in our popular media. The following volume is an exploration into our complex relationship with the forest as a geographical and ecological context, as it is rendered in myth, media and legend. While few of the chapters in this text will offer direct insights into ecology or biology, the content within explores the ways in which media represents forests and the creatures that inhabit them.

The collection begins with *Part 1: Ferocious Forests* which provides a series of discussions around the forest as context and subject – a domain that contains monsters and is itself monstrous. This first part begins with Richard Mills' discussion of the pastoral horrors of British horror films, such as *The Blood on Satan's Claw* (1971) and *The Devil Rides Out* (1968), and their influence on iconographies around haunted or monstrous forests in more recent media. To exemplify his discussion, Mills provides a detailed semiotic analysis of the 'Night Witch' music video by Wolf People (2016). This analysis offers the reader an understanding of established Pagan and horror iconographies located in wooded spaces.

This chapter is followed by Elizabeth Parker's chapter "'That Awful Secret of the Wood": Venturing Beneath the Deep Dark Forest'. Here Parker analyses gothic literature and horror film, and the vague terms with which arboreal horrors are discussed within these texts – their innately illusive character. Rather than being inhabited by specific, characterised monsters, the gothic forest is innately monstrous and threatening. Indeed, the forest becomes a foreboding 'landscape of fear' within these texts, which continually refer to a 'something' in the woods. What this something is, Parker posits, is that awful secret of the wood, hidden within and underneath the haunted forest.

Part 1 is brought to a close with András Fodor's chapter, which offers a detailed discussion of Brian Catling's *The Vorrh* (2016). The name The Vorrh within the novel refers to a great sacred forest, cohabited by gods, humans and monstrous apparitions. Fodor discusses *The Vorrh*'s ability to disrupt conventional perceptions of time and space both for the reader and within the story. In contrast to The Vorrh within the story – as a primordial and undeveloped space – is the city of Essenwald, a colonizing transplant from Europe that is positioned in a curious symbiosis.

The second section of the collection examines more specific denizens of these dark woods and begins with Jon Hackett's discussion of the representational practices resulting from the use of practical effects in werewolf films. This relationship, between technology and transformation, being central to the cycle of werewolf films beginning in the 1980s, informs the heyday of werewolf films to date; in terms of the number of films produced and the critical success of the transformations and mutations depicted within. Hackett's account integrates detailed analyses of the werewolf films of this period to more contemporary examples, and in a similar fashion charts the dawn to the dusk of the use of practical special effects.

Benjamin Dalton's chapter theorises the significance of forest realms in the cinema and fiction of Alain Guiraudie. He begins with a theoretical exposition of the possible articulation of queer theory with ecology, using the work of Catherine Malabou on plasticity as a framework. The chapter then proceeds to a close textual analysis of Guiraudie's cinema in relation to these concepts, considering the significance of forests as a site of queer becoming for the protagonists of the films. In relation to Guiraudie's widely admired *Stranger by the Lake* (2013), for instance, the forest is deemed to promise 'untapped potentiality for queer revival, reinvention and rewilding'. This will involve new forms of community between its human, non-human and inorganic constituents.

Alexander Sergeant provides us with a psychoanalytic interpretation of the significance of the forest in contemporary fantasy film and fiction. Acknowledging such precursors as Bruno Bettelheim's psychoanalytic readings of fairy tales, Sergeant proposes instead a Kleinian framework that avoids reductive readings in terms of dream symbolism; and better integrates the working of phantasy in forest narratives with the claims of the reality principle. Through discussion of a number of recent fantasy films, the fruitfulness of this interpretive model is made clear in an engaging discussion of the significance of filmic forests, whether 'good' or 'bad' in Kleinian terms.

The final section of the volume continues the collection's ruminations on the cultural significance of the forest, through studies that together constitute a case-study on the work of J.R.R. Tolkien. Brad Eden opens this section with a consideration of the importance of trees in his legendarium, contextualising the discussion in reference to recent scholarship that has highlighted 'different aspects and uses of trees in the daily life, worship, and understanding of ancient and medieval British and Anglo-Saxon society'. Tolkien's evident familiarity with mythical precedents informs his treatment of trees, making links between modern and earlier reverence for them; Eden discusses this particularly in relation to the most recently published of the author's works.

Leticia Cortina Aracil turns her attention to the liminal spaces of the forest in Tolkien's works – and the role that the forest takes as comparable to the underworld in other myths and legends. She untertakes a close textual analysis of Tolkien's works in order to elucidate the pivotal scenes in his fiction in which the forests themselves intervene as agents for the other characters. As well as providing sites of existential significance and trans-formation for human and humanoid characters, the forests occupy a cosmo-logical role too, linking particular narrative events to wider mythological contexts from within the legendarium.

Finally, Damian O'Byrne's chapter completes the section – and the volume – while continuing the examination of trees and their significance in Tolkien's legendarium. Analysis of Tolkien's works and letters leads O'Byrne to conclude that trees present more ambiguous figures in his oeuvre than frequently envisaged, both hostile and friendly to the novels' protago-nists, sometimes evolving from one to the other across successive drafts of the same work. The analysis is brought up to date with a poignant discussion of the demise of 'Tolkien's Tree' earlier this decade. The devotee of Tolkien will find much of interest, therefore, in the chapters by Eden, Cortina Aracil and O'Byrne that close this collection.

Bibliography

Adams, James Eli (2018) 'Monstrosity' in *Victorian Literature and Culture*, Volume 46, Issue 3–4 Fall/Winter 2018 , pp. 776–779.

Adorno, T. and Horkheimer, M. (1944) *The Dialectics of Enlightenment*, Stanford: Stanford University Press.

Althusser, L. (1971) *Lenin and Philosophy*, New York, Monthly Review.

Apostle (2018) Dir. Evans, Gareth [Film] USA: XYZ Films.

Asma, S.T. (2009), *On Monsters: An Unnatural History of Our Worst Fears*, Oxford & New York. Oxford University Press.

Bruegel, Jan (1605) *Belebte Waldstraße* [Oil on Canvas] Bavarian State Painting Collections, Munich.

Catling, B. (2016). *The Vorrh*, London: Hodder & Stoughton.

Cole, Laura (2018) 'Outlawed logging: saving the primeval forests of Poland' Available at: http://geo-graphical.co.uk/places/forests/item/2743-outlawed-logging

Dark (2017) Creators: bo Odar, Baran & Friese, Jantje [Television Series] Germany: Wiedemann & Berg Television.

Forbrydelsen (2007) Dir. Larsen, Birger [Television Series] Denmark: DR.

Grimm (2011–) Prod. Kouf, Jim et al. [Television Series] USA: Universal Television.

La Forêt (2017) Dir. Berg, Julius [Television Series] France: France 3.

Nature (2018) 'Brazil's new president adds to global threat to science' in *Nature* 563, pp. 5–6 (2018).

Nelson, Arthur (2017) 'Donald Trump 'taking steps to abolish Environmental Protection Agency'' Available at: https://www.theguardian.com/us-news/2017/feb/02/donald-trump-plans-to-abolish-en-vironmental-protection-agency.

Ringel, Faye (2017) 'Early American Gothic (Puritan and New Republic)' in *The Cambridge Companion to American Gothic*, UK: Cambridge University Press, pp. 15–30.

Sabrina (2018–) Prod. Forrest, Craig et al. [Television Series] USA: Warner Bros.

The Blood on Satan's Claw (1971) Dir. Haggard, Piers [Film] UK: Tigon British Film.

The Devil Rides Out (1968) Dir. Fischer, Terence [Film] UK: Hammer Film Productions.

The Killing (2011–2014) Producers: Zelman, Aaron, Doner, Jeremy and Campo, Kirsten [Television Series] USA: Fox Television Studios.

The Ritual (2017) Dir. Bruckner, David [Film] UK: eOne Films.

The Witch (2015) Dir. Eggers, Robert [Film] USA: Parts and Labour.

The X-Files (1993–2002) Creator: Carter, Chris [Television Series] USA: Fox.

Twin Peaks (1990–1991) Creators: Lynch, David & Frost, Mark [Television Series] USA: Lynch/Frost Productions.

Wolf People (2016), *Night Witch*, Jagjaguwar [Single].

Wright, A. (2013), *Monstrosity: The Human Monster in Visual Culture*, London. I.B. Tauris.

Żmihorski, Michał, Chylarecki, Przemysław, Orczewska, Anna and Wesołowski, Tomasz (2018) 'Białowieża Forest: A new threat' in *Science* 6399, Vol. 361, p. 238.

Part 1

Ferocious Forests

Chapter 1

'You're already in Hell': Representations of the Forest in Wolf People's video *Night Witch* (2016)

Richard Mills

My paper will discuss the representations of the forest in Wolf People's *Night Witch* video, which was released in 2016. The imagery of the forest is reminiscent of British folk horror: the panorama shots of the pagan scenery in *The Wicker Man* (1973), the camp horror of Tigon's *The Blood on Satan's Claw* (1971) and Hammer's *The Devil Rides Out* (1968), and the anti-pastoral savagery of *Kill List* (2011). The video employs the conceit of found footage of the forest, resembling the evocations of the woods in the *The Blair Witch Project* (1999) and *Cannibal Holocaust* (1980). The Wolf People logo, a 'W' made out of twigs, recurs in the video and is influenced by the stick people that appear nailed to trees in *The Blair Witch Project*.

As we will see, *Night Witch* is a video that is part of a resurgence in electric English folk horror; bands such as These New Puritans, P.J. Harvey and Bishi. The *Night Witch* video is also part of contemporary folk horror where an eerie anthropocene landscape raises discomfort about the contemporary body politic and environmental concerns. The combination of music and film in *Night Witch*, can be seen as a kind of social map that tracks the unconscious ley lines between a huge range of different forms of media in the twentieth century and earlier. It is one that connects the past and the present to create a clash of belief systems and people; modernity and Enlightenment against superstition and faith; the very violence inherent within us as people. It is the evil under the soil, the terror in the backwoods or the forgotten land, the loneliness in the brutalist tower block, and the ghosts that haunt stones and patches of dark, lonely water. It is both nostalgic for and questioning days gone by, romantic in its allure of a more open society's ways, but realistic in its honesty surrounding their ultimate prejudice and violence. It is tales of hours dreadful and strange, a media that requires a literal walking and traversing to fully understand its inner workings (Scovell, 2017, p. 183).

Scovell's description of folk horror sketches the aesthetic of *Night Witch's* depopulated and disquieting English landscape. However the horror tropes have a political unconscious: the *Night Witch* video uses stereotypical horror imagery of the *unheimlich*, which hints at wider societal concerns:

> A sense of the eerie seldom clings to enclosed and inhabited domestic spaces; we find the eerie more readily in landscapes partially emptied of the human. What happened to produce these ruins, this disappearance? […] These questions can be posed in a psychoanalytical register – if we are not who we think we are, what are we? – but they also apply to the forces governing capitalist society. Capital is at every level an eerie entity – conjured out of nothing – capital nevertheless exerts more influence than any allegedly substantial entity (Fisher, 2016, p. 11).

The swooping *Evil Dead* aerial shots, *The Blair Witch* wicker crosses, the semi-human white sheet figures and the haunting wind rippling across the water of *Night Witch's* depopulated and anthropocene landscape is all in the tradition of folk horror, but the eeriness and emptiness of the landscape is about the haunting of capital or lack thereof, as well as Gothic horror metaphor for environmental catastrophe.

Horror films are subversive in the sense that they reject English heritage versions of a safe and reactionary rural idyll. Landscape in the music and videos of Wolf People becomes 'a violent collision between present and past, between conventionally different realms of discourse (art and politics in particular)' (Macdonald Daly, 2009, p. xix). The English countryside is defamiliarised in *Night Witch* in a similar manner to a scene in Ellis Sharp's short story *The Hay Wain* (1992); the central character of this story, Robinson, is fleeing police after the 1990 Poll Tax Riots in Trafalgar Square. As Robinson is being pursued, he stops to view Constable's *The Hay Wain*, the symbol of English landscape heritage:

> much bigger than he'd imagined after seeing it all those times on biscuit tins and trays and calendars and hanging on the lounge wall of remote dusty relatives along with the Reader's Digest Novels and the 22" TV and the hideous china and country maids and cherry-cheeked grinning shepherds' (Sharp 2009, p. 137).

This famous work of art by England's greatest landscape painter is subverted in a similar fashion to the folk horror of Ben Wheatley's *Kill List* and Wolf People's *Night Witch*. As the police arrest Robinson, they throw him against the picture with his blood, 'spurting in a bright unreal slash across *The Hay Wain* by John Constable R.A.' (Sharp, 2009, p. 141).

Night Witch subverts the English rural idyll landscape in their video in a similar way to Sharp's character in *The Hay Wain*. Instead of blood on the canvas; the director Balaeva, employs *arbre misérable* instead of blood to achieve an anti-pastoral horror-scape. Trees and the forest are the primary focus in the video. Arboreal beauty is destroyed by witches' crosses in the forest, cameras speeding through woods creating a sense of panic and pursuit, and shadowy and dark spectral trees that are reminiscent of malnourished Giacometti figures. The Wolf People 'W' logo is nailed to trees in the style of *The Blair Witch Project*, and the glades in the wood have small crosses strewn on the ground and on the trees making the woods look as if they are covered in the detritus of a pagan and satanic coven. Sharp has Robinson's blood splash on the epitome of English heritage, *The Hay Wain*, and rather like the Chapman brothers. Jake and Dinos Chapman, Sharp's fiction and Wolf People's video have bloodied the English countryside. Jonathan Jones explains:

> Two years ago, the Chapmans bought a complete set of what has become the most revered series of prints in existence, Goya's *Disasters of War*. It is a first-rate, mint condition set of 80 etchings printed from the artist's plates. In terms of print connoisseurship, in terms of art history, in any terms, this is a treasure – and they have vandalised it (*The Guardian*, 2003).

The Chapman brothers called their work *The Rape of Creativity* and they 'changed all the visible victims' heads to clowns' heads and puppies' heads' (*The Guardian*, 2003). Their intention with the clowns and puppy heads was to remove any liberal humanist romance about war and violence from the prints. It is a method similar to the horror movie aesthetic concerning the countryside: Wolf People use horror tropes to change tourist brochures into a post-modernist nightmare. The Chapman Brothers explain:

> So one reason for altering 80 original Goya prints is that it may finally offend the people the Chapmans see as their target – an audience in which they include themselves; the liberal, humanist, gallery-going chattering classes. (When asked whom he sees as the enemy, Jake says "Dinos".) It worked on me, when I first heard about it. After all, Goya's Disasters of War is not some dry old relic no one cares about – it is a work that has never lost its power to shock (*The Guardian*, 2003).

The strangely depopulated and unnerving *Night Witch* video is an example of what Mark Fisher calls 'eerie Thanatos'. As the video develops the viewers' eyes are drawn to an anthropocene landscape in which there are no organic life and no human figures. The video is infused with an eerie non-human death drive of pagan nature. There is an all-pervading sense of folk horror in the woods, on stone cairns and even skimming across the surface of a huge lake. To Fisher, this is

> a drive of death. The inorganic is the impersonal pilot of everything, including that which seems to be personal and 7organic. Seen from the perspective of Thanatos, we ourselves become an exemplary case of the eerie: there is an agency in us (the unconscious, the death drive), but it is not where or what we expect it to be' (Fisher, 2016, p. 85).

As we shall see, the eerie in *Night Witch* uses a disembodied camera swooping over an unsettled and unsettling English landscape which leads to viewers intuiting and meditating on environmental and political concerns: Hammer horror ironic fear and Ben Wheatley-like terror has stimulated a psychological process where thoughts may grow; and the angular jarring electric folk music is a perfect complement to this contemporary folk horror piece.

The *Night Witch* video uses panorama shots of a non-human landscape which is haunted by ghostly spectres in the form of shadows and in one scene a ghostly image of what appears to be a witch on a broom stick flicks across the screen. It looks like a human figure but the shadow is so fleeting and amorphous that the view cannot be sure. These rapid aerial shots evoke *The Wicker Man* as they have the effect of rendering nature as powerful, pagan and unusual: nature without people. In *The Wicker Man*, people look insect-like and insignificant; and in *Night Witch* the absence of human beings shows a landscape remote and autonomous from anthropomorphic presences. These bird's eye shots evoke a supernatural effect: nature is uncanny and malevolent, but the metaphysics of the video use unsettling paganism to establish existentialism and atheism. There is no supernatural realm: nature is uncanny and strange without adding mysticism to the mix.

The video is an example of an anthropocene text, which means there are no human presences in the film. It is also a non-narrative video, where the visuals are mostly autonomous in relation to the sound and lyrics. Another technical feature of the film is helicopter shots (and drone cameras) which achieve an *Evil Dead* (1981) effect of charging through the woods at an accelerated and convulsive pace.

Anamorphosis, an abstracted stain on the visual field, is employed in this video. As such, the imagery is at times reminiscent of Holbein's Renaissance painting *The Ambassadors*, where an elongated and abstracted skull (*a memento mori*) is placed at the bottom of the painting as a visual puzzle. The viewer must approach the painting from an acute angle to be able to see the distorted anamorphic image. To Lacan, the anamorphosis in *The Ambassadors* represents Thanatos, the death drive; he writes: 'Begin by walking out of the room [...] it is then that, turning around as you leave [...] you apprehend in this form ... what? A skull? Holbein makes visible for us here something which is simply the subject as annihilated' (Lacan, 1981, p. 88).

Night Witch applies this symbol of 'a skull representing annihilation' to a black and grey contorted witch's shawl in the foreground of one shot and a twisting sheet in another: these images take on a three dimensional effect, which accustoms the viewers' eyes to an uncanny non-human presence, and very importantly adds an anti-pastoral element to the text. Nature is depicted as malevolent and dangerous, and the supernatural is galvanised paradoxically to convey a pagan atheism. The video convinces that God is dead, but our minds, and eyes, are assaulted with unsettling series of non-Christian images that are designed convey that Hell is in the here and now.

The video is has the quality of an hallucination: an English pagan landscape which visualises evil lingering in nature and it is our anthropomorphic sensibility which creates human forms in the piece – for example, it takes repeated views to notice the silhouette of a witch on a broomstick at 1.34 in the video. Even this, shape is amorphous and it is left to the view to create the shape of a human figure. The lyrics help the viewers to visualise this animated Rorschach card, with its invocation of 'wings of paper and wood' and its visual opposition of snow and 'cold blackness'.

The cover of the album *Ruins*, on which *Night Witch* appears, is noteworthy. It is in this English supernatural tradition (Wolf People's atheist subtext notwithstanding) – it is a tarot-card knight with his head bowed with a black ink drawing of a Giacometti-thin tree which is flanked by two dark figures which are reminiscent of a medieval woodcut. Above these two figures is the Wolf People typography with its *Blair Witch*-style W and its two O's in the style of the international Venus sign; this Wolf People logo is a visual trope along with the gender sign, which appear throughout the video.

The *Ruins* album cover and the Night Witch video are influenced by the supernatural symbolism of H. P. Lovecraft, Arthur Symons and the Hermetic philosophy and magic of the Order of the Golden Dawn – whose members included Bram Stoker, W. B. Yeats, and Aleister Crowley. *Night Witch* invokes these supernatural influences, but the mysticism is a strangely depopulated atheistic paganism. This supernatural English landscape is also a twisted pastoral: a heavy metal Vaughan Williams; in fact, the powerful electric music is English nostalgia that in an age of cyberspace harks back to the past of the folk rock of the late 1960s and the early 1970s. Rob Young elucidates this nostalgic tendency:

> In an age of rapid change, nostalgia and revivalism often flourish: they offer solace of permanence and stability in a world whose certainties seem to be slipping away. British innovation is habitually shadowed by restoration; the Victorian mania for building schools, factories, churches and municipal buildings was couched in the architectural vernacular of medieval Gothic. Vaughan Williams, to a lesser extent Holst, and the younger composers of the English pastoral school envisioned [...] a future for British music woven with rich threads of its past (Young 2010, p. 76).

In a sense, Wolf People's *Night Witch* is a violent English anti-pastoral which is the antithesis of Vaughan Williams's *Lark Ascending* (1914); *Night Witch* is the opposite of Williams's ethereal lark invoking a utopian English landscape. Wolf People use electric guitars to create disquiet and disharmony with nature; Williams, on the other hand, uses a melodious and soaring violin to magic up images of green fields and a rural idyll of man and nature in perfect harmony. When the rapid camera movement of *The Evil Dead* (1981) and the aerial shots of *The Wicker Man* are combined with music that evokes Black Sabbath and the folk rock of Led Zeppelin III, we have a wicked mélange of contemporary anti-pastoral, atheistic, pagan music.

Night Witch is a secular and aesthetic text which is a visual performance of jumbled reality and occultist imagery. The video is a Gothic horror piece which conveys the idea that there is no supernatural realm: our reality is comprised of hallucinogenic psychosis and subatomic weirdness; and *Night Witch* is a film that uses stock horror leitmotifs to communicate the political point that we should build a paradise in this Hell: 'turn this cold blackness to light'. In fact Gothic horror, and in particular the anti-pastoralism, is political art, as Robert MacFarlane, puts it:

> What is under way, across a broad spectrum of culture, is an attempt to account for the turbulence of England in the era of late capitalism. The supernatural and paranormal have always been means of figuring powers that cannot otherwise find visible expression. Contemporary anxieties and dissents are here being reassembled and re-presented as spectres, shadows or monsters: our noun monster, indeed, shares an etymology with our verb to demonstrate, meaning to show or reveal (with a largely lost sense of omen or portent) (*The Guardian*, 2015).

The *Night Witch* video is informed by an eerie absence: an anthropocene presence of being watched, but not being able to see any human figures apart from in a very amorphous and abstract human form. Again this is a nuanced and unconsciously political piece of art implying ecological and political concerns: the landscape is being concreted over at an alarming rate and there are British citizens relying on food banks; viewed in this context this video is hauntingly political. The English countryside is about our current fears and concerns:

> We are, certainly, very far from 'nature writing' [...] and into a mutated cultural terrain that includes the weird and the punk as well as the attentive and the devotional. Among the shared landmarks of this terrain are ruins, fields, pits, fringes, relics, buried objects, hilltops, falcons, demons and deep pasts. In much of this work, suppressed forces pulse and flicker beneath the ground and within the air (capital, oil, energy, violence, state power, surveillance), waiting to erupt or to condense

> This terrain to Robert Farlane is 'the idea of an English eerie – 'the skull beneath the skin of the countryside'. And this art for a new generation this has nothing to do with hokey supernaturalism – it's a cultural and political response to contemporary crises and fears (The Guardian, 2015).

The twisted ghost's shape and vaguely human amorphous witch shape are predicated on folk horror such as *The Blood on Satan's Claw* (1971) and *The Devil Rides Out* (1968). Rob Young describes Piers Haggard's *Blood On Satan's Claw*:

when a camera tracks the gouging of a 17th century ploughman's blade through crumbly soil. Out of the earth emerges a grisly skull, with fur attached and a functioning eyeball. It promptly disappears, never to be found again, but its malefic influence begins to work in insidious ways upon the village. Mysterious fur patches appear on limbs; a claw bursts out of a wooden floor; fevers and hysteria spread through the population as it becomes clearer that the Devil is attempting to incarnate himself on earth (*Uncut*, 2013).

The cinematography is very reminiscent of *Night Witch*: dark, Gothic gloom and red erotic lips of the protagonist framed by pastoral greens. We can see the influence of the *The Devil Rides Out* (1968) on *Night Witch* – the silhouette of a witch of a broomstick and the devil with a goat's head and body of a man perched superciliously on a rock-cum-altar in the English forest.

The violent and terrifying English landscape of Ben Wheatley's *Kill List* (2011) also permeates each shot in *Night Witch*. The *Blair Witch* crosses portentously frame every shot of the video. *The Guardian*'s Peter Bradshaw describes Wheatley' silm as 'an occult chiller with shades of *Wicker Man* and *Blair Witch* – and be warned right now: there are some ultra-violent and infra-retch scenes that have had people making for the exits. I wondered if director Ben Wheatley considered putting a death metal version of Maxwell's Silver Hammer over the closing credits' (*The Guardian* 2011). Bradshaw could be describing the anti-pastoral photography of *Kill List*: pitch black backgrounds illuminated by figures in wicker masks holding burning stakes. In a manner similar to *Night Witch*, *Kill List* is a contemporary disquieting and forest in the English countryside.

Will Ashon's work on forests is useful for putting this kind of aesthetic film analysis in a political context. The magic of the forests in *Night Witch* and *Kill List* is a radical critique of capitalism; quoting Francis Bacon he contends that, 'by breaking the idea of the body as "receptacle of magic powers" – and instead turning it into a Cartesian meat-machine for work – were the conditions for capitalism fulfilled. It was Francis Bacon who said that "Magic kills industry"' (Ashon, 2017, p. 315). The aerial shots of forests and the wicker masks and voodoo dolls on the trees in the woods in Night Witch are eco-paganism of the English landscape which conveys unease at the state of the nation.

The landscape in *Night Witch* is a deserted horror dystopia which recalls two other contemporary English musicians: P.J. Harvey and Bishi, both artists who use the trope of the anti-pastoral English landscape, and English folk music history and tradition, to make commentary about the violence of contemporary society. In the video for P.J. Harvey's *Let England Shake* images of England have the same authorial intention as *Night Witch*. The visual horror tropes in *Night Witch* convey a spooky landscape to hint at disquiet; and the juxtaposition of semiotic signs in *Let England Shake* does the same. The video begins with a rural man with a West Country accent reading the lyrics to the song; then a deserted fairground; punch and Judy dolls fighting, a sinister Hammer horror close up of Mr Punch grinning satanically, and these anti-pastoral signs are put together with a pastoral English landscape of grey skies, waves breaking on beaches and wide, silver seascapes. The series of landscape images provokes political uneasiness in a similar manner as *Night Witch*. Gardner contends that the spaces that we see and imagine in *Let England Shake* are an England of fogs, graveyards, the Thames, the white cliffs of Dover, ploughed fields and dead sea-captains. This is arguably an 'old' England, a collage of historical and politically important landscapes and literary characters that have peopled prose, poetry and song over many centuries. However, Harvey uses this heritage as a background on which she maps tales of war and brutality and sutures into that map songs of soldiers reminiscing about 'home' (Gardner, 2017, p. 77).

The video for *Let England Shake* is in the carnival Hammer horror tradition which turns the English pastoral tradition on its head by providing a series of freakish images of the English landscape which rejects English heritage culture.

Bishsi's video for *Albion Voice* is in the subversive anti-pastoral tradition of *Night Witch* as well. Although *Albion Voice* does not have the eerie horror of *Night Witch*, the video juxtaposes 'villages green', cathedrals, and 'old England's dream' landscape with shots of Bishi dressed as Queen Elizabeth II, the white cliffs of Dover, wearing a Union Jack dress and a bodice, dancing in green fields, and playing a sitar in a green English landscape to convey the point that national identity is a hybrid of different cultures (in her case, Indian and English). The refrain of the song drives the point home that cultural and identity is a mess of interlocking strains, 'Indian skin/Albion voice' (*Albion Voice*, 2012). Simon Keegan-Philips and Trish Winter describe this 'third-space' (Bhabha, 1994) in the following terms:

> When Bishi sings, 'bewildering world' (in the chorus and outro of 'Albion Voice'), the word 'bewildering' is accented, elongated and ornamented: the performance, however, is one of an artist in secure control of the multiple contradictions and tropes she calls up. She seems to be embracing the potentially 'bewildering' multiplicity of identities, just as they are embraced in her work though her multiple costume changes, many impersonations of iconic historical English and British national icons, and the multiple Bishis of her kaleidoscopic image projections (Simon Keegan-Philips and Trish Gardner, 2017, p. 205).

When the *Night Witch* video is seen in the context of the *Let England Shake* and the *Albion Voice* videos, the commonality here is that all three pieces of work are using disquieting and freakish images of the English landscape to depict societal concerns about economic disparity, national identity post-Brexit and the environment. *The Night Witch* video eschews the dominant English heritage rural idyll version of the landscape. Mark Fisher cites Patrick Keiller's notes from before the filming of the latter's *Robinson in*

Ruins (2010), arguing that the rural landscape is always already intensely politicised,

> I had embarked on landscape film making in 1981, early in the Thatcher era, after encountering a surrealist tradition in the UK and elsewhere, so that cinematography involved the pursuit of a transformation, radical or otherwise of everyday reality [...] I had forgotten that landscape photography is often motivated by utopian or imperatives, both as a critique of the world, and to demonstrate the possibility of creating a better one (Keiller, cited in Fisher, 2104, p. 226)

Balaeva's video employs eerie found footage reminiscent of *The Blair Witch Project's* conceit of the viewers watching the missing cameraman's footage after he has mysteriously vanished. The same conceit of finding a dead cameraman's footage is used in *Cannibal Holocaust*; this found footage idea is used to shock viewers into re-thinking any idealistic preconceptions of a heritage landscape: the horrifically transformed depopulated and pagan English landscape of *Night Witch* is the id of an English political unconscious.

Although *Night Witch* looks back to the traditional British horror such as *The Wicker Man*, it is a thoroughly contemporary piece of transgressive pagan filmmaking such as *Kill List* (2011) and *A Field in England* (2013) and it is recalls the contemporary pagan folk music of These New Puritans, whose music conveys spectral emptiness and haunting non-spaces very similar to the eerie sound and visual stylings of Wolf People. Ben Wheatley contends that this pagan interest is flourishing *de nos jours*:

> A lot gets read into film history. You have to think about where the Hammer films come from and where *The Wicker Man* comes from. In North America, you might not get this, but in the UK this stuff is old. It's old, old, in-the-Earth-sort-of-stuff. So if this makes sense, I'm referencing the same stuff those films are referencing, but I'm not referencing those films. I'm not thinking, 'Wouldn't it be neat to re-do *The Wicker Man.*' I live in Brighton, on the coast, and there's this town called Lewes that does this famous fireworks display. And it's all very pagan. People come around, they dress up in these strange costumes and burn crosses and barrels and this effigy of the Pope that they set aflame. So stuff like that still goes on (Nayman, 2013).

The English landscape of *Night Witch* is shot in a panoramic and dynamic manner, which is key to the subversive nature of this piece of film making. Writing about the English singer and songwriter Nick Drake, Nathan Wiseman-Trowse captures the disruptive quality of this transgressive video:

> Movement and transition are key to understanding Drake's music, in that he represents moments of negotiation and conciliation between competing mythologies of English character. Drake's Englishness is far from the mythological England trapped forever under glass; rather, his music

represents us with negotiating the tensions between Romanticism and Modernity (Trowse, 2013, p. 68).

The tensions in *Night Witch* are the occultist imagery of wicker crosses and spooky aerial shots which defamiliarise a heritage English landscape and communicate a strained and disturbing land in constant flux. In fact the mysterious and supernatural quality of this film is 'a *terra nullis*, a nothing place, [...] this is a region whose breadth seems to return the eye's enquiries unanswered, or to swallow attempts at interpretation' (MacFarlane, 2015, p. 16). The anthropocene landscape that has no discernible human life (apart from shadowy preternatural silhouettes) and no band members from Wolf People, is a depopulated landscape that is a signifier of eco-doom, an harbinger of political stasis and a statement about personal paralysis in a changing and vital horrorscape:

> The truth is, our minds are much more like forests than they are fields, dark and labyrinthine, with sudden clearings where the light is so bright you can hardly see, then shadow and dead leaves and green moss and the husks of nuts and seeds scattered beneath trees, the sound of wind through the branches. We don't find ourselves on a dark forest in the middle of our lives, we realise we've always been there. We see ourselves-finally after all these years!-and what we see is neither tidy nor rational, neither orderly nor static. It's what we do that matters. We can decide to run from it, marching out following a straight line. We can attempt to raze it to the ground and replant it in the hope that we will make it more productive. Or we can try to get to know the terrain better, appreciate its oddities, its uniqueness, try to get a feel for our own strange and boring, beautiful and ugly, our enclosed and unenclosable life (Ashon, 2017, p. 341).

Wolf People are, as the music journalist Tom Cox puts it, 'light, bright people who sing about dark events: four scruffy, polite men in their 30s who know their Pentangle from their Pentagram, and, via blasts of fuzz guitar, sweaty funk blues drumming, pastoral melody and a folklorist's sense of storytelling, are on a mission to evoke a magical – and often brutal – rural England that is under-represented in modern song writing' (*The Guardian*, 2013).

Wolf People are concerned about writing about the English landscape in a visual way. The lyrics of the song are a gift for a film maker: tree stumps, flying witches, broomsticks, death, cold, paper and wood wings: 'I'm really surprised that people today don't write more about their surroundings and people other than themselves' says their lead singer Jack Sharp, 'One of the things that draws me to folk music is that it's so illustrative and diverse. It throws up pictures while you listen' (*The Guardian*, 2013).

Wolf People's work is in the tradition of 1960s and 1970s electric folk rock. Bands who have influenced them are the hard rock groups such as Black Sabbath, Led Zeppelin and Thin Lizzy; and the folk rock of Fairport

Convention, Pentangle and The Incredible String Band. The folk finger-picking traditional music of Anne Briggs and Shirley Collins is also clearly discernible in their work. Wolf People also add a contemporary rock feel to these artists with clear, sharp production and crisp pauses between phrases which makes their sound cleaner and more spacious than muddier sixties and seventies records. Perhaps the song that *Night Witch* most resembles is Bubble Puppy's *Lonely* (1969); Bubble Puppy were an American psychedelic rock band originally active from 1967 to 1972. They are best remembered for their Top 20 hit, *Hot Smoke & Sasafrass* (1969). In a style similar to Night Witch, *Lonely* has two dueting rock guitars that make an elliptical and staccato sound. Both songs alternate the volume throughout which adds tension between each guitar phrase. These folk rock spaces of *Night Witch* and *Lonely* are ideal for building frames around in a film.

The lineage of Wolf People's art is very clear both musically and visually: psychedelic electric folk music and English folk horror movies. The word folk drives from 'Volk' in ancient Teutonic and Wolf People videos (see the *When the Fire is Dead in the Grate*) are built on an unsettling wooded sense of mystery:

> The Volk's playground was the Wald: the forest that looms with such powerful, murky force in so many European myths and fairy tales. The Teutonic root of 'Wald' – 'walthus' – is an ancestor of both 'wood' and 'wild'. Seen from a German perspective, then, the word 'folk' feels inextricably wedded to Northern Europe's barbarous wooded interior. The Roman Empire cleared away much of the forest during its European campaigns, but the Nordic wildness survives in any English place name ending with 'wald', 'wold' or 'weald'. Other curiosities survive too; things of which we have only a limited understanding. By the second half of the twentieth century folk culture in Britain had become a kind of cargo cult, a jumble of disassociated local customs, rituals and superstitions: uncanny relics of the distant, unknowable Britain of ancient days (Young, 2010, pp. 181–182).

The term psychogeography describes the folk aesthetics of the Night Witch video and song as the empty landscape and rock textures are a profound negotiation between people's psyches and place. Both texts have their primordial origins in rural Bedfordshire and Wolf People's beginnings were in a small Bedfordshire village which the 2011 census calculates to be 1,750 and with such a rural influence the song writing in Wolf People is drawn to quiet back waters that are surrounded by the noise and tumult of twenty-first century southern England.

The stain between the old and new is the core of Night Witch's folk horror; 'Folk songs existed in constant transformation, a living example of an art form in a perpetual state of renewal' (Young, 2010, p. 67). They have adapted their various influences into a strange anthropocene text that with tropes of empty open spaces, haunted woods and threat of impending violence and menace ensure that the English folk tradition in cinema and song is a mutable stream of fresh art that doesn't lose sight of its roots. Wolf People's *Night Witch* video looks back and mines stock images of English horror and musical phrases of psychedelic rock in order to be in the vanguard of new English music: Wolf People look back to move forward. *Night Witch* is an anthropocene text which warns of a dire future unless there is a political address to our present calamities. It uses occultist imagery as an eco-warning and also to demonstrate that we are in the here and now and that the only ghosts that exists are real fears which haunt the labyrinthine woods of our minds.

Bibliography

Ashon, W, (2017), *Strange Labyrinth: Outlaws, Poets, Mystics, Murders and a Coward in London's Great Forest*, Granta.

Balaeva, M. (2016), Dir. Wolf People's *Night Witch*.

Bhabha, H.K. (1994), *The Location of Culture*, London: Routledge.

Bishi (2012), *Albion Voice* [CD] Gryphon.

Bishi (2012), *Bishiworld*, 4 January. Available online: http://bishiworld.blogspot.co.uk/2012_04_01_archive.html. Accessed 08/09/2018.

Bubble (1969), Lonely on *A Gathering of Promises* [Album].

Cox, T. 'Folk Songs are there to tell a story', *The Guardian*. https://www.theguardian.com/music/2013/jul/21/wolf-people-fain-interview accessed 08/09/2018.

*Cannibal Holocaust (*1980), [Film] Dir. Deodato, R., Italy: Shameless.

Evil Dead (1981), Dir. [Film] Raimi, S. (1981), D., USA: Studiocanal.

Fisher, M. (2014), *Ghosts of My Life: Writings on Depression, Hauntology and Lost Futures,* Zero Books: UK and USA.

Fisher, M. (2016), *The Weird and the Eerie*, Repeater: London.

Gardner, A. (2017), 'PJ Harvey and remembering England' in *Mad Dogs and Englishness: Popular Music and English Identities* (eds), Brooks, Donnelly and Mills, Bloomsbury: New York.

Haggard, P. (1971), Dir. *The Blood on Satan's Claw*.

Hardy, R. (1973), Dir. *The Wicker Man*.

Harvey, P. J. (2011) *Let England Shake*, Island Records [Album].

Keegan-Philips, S. and Winter, T. (2017), 'Albion Voice: The Englishness of Bishi' in *Mad Dogs and Englishness: Popular Music and English Identities* (eds), Brooks, Donnelly and Mills, Bloomsbury: New York.

Keiller, P (2010), Dir. *Robinson in Ruins Kill List* (2011), [Film] Dir. Wheatley, B., UK: Studiocanal.

Lacan, J. (1981), *The Four Fundamental Concepts of Psychoanalysis*, W.W. Norton and Company: New York and London.

Lark Ascending (2014), Williams, V., UK: Decca.

Led Zeppelin, *Led Zeppelin III* (1970), Atlantic [Album].

Let England Shake: 12 Short Films (2011), [Short Film] Dir. Murphy S., UK: Island.

Macfarlane, R. (2015), *Landmarks*, Penguin Books, London.

Macfarlane, R. (2015), 'The Eeriness of the English Countryside', *The Guardian*, https://www.theguardian.com/books/2015/apr/10/eeriness-english-countryside-robert-macfarlane. Accessed 06/09/2018.

Nayman, A. (2013) 'Hammer Horror: Ben Wheatley's Kill List' in http://cinemascope.com/cinemascope-magazine/interviews-hammer-horror-ben-wheatleys-kill-list-by-adam-nayman. Accessed 09/09/2018.

Scovell, A. (2017), Folk Horror: *Hours Dreadful and Things Strange*, Columbia University Press: New York.

Sharp, E. (2009), MacDonald Daly's Introduction to *Dead Iraqis*, Critical, Cultural and Communications Press: London.

The Blair Witch Project (1999) [Film] Dir. Myrick, D. and Sanchez, E., USA: Pathé.

These New Puritans (2013), *Field of Reeds* [Album].

Wiseman, T. (2013), *Nick Drake: Dreaming England*, Reaktion Books: Glasgow.

Wolf People (2014) *When the Fire is Dead in the Grate*, Dir. Wolf People.

Wolf People (2016), *Ruins,* Jagjaguwar [Album].

Wolf People (2016), *Night Witch*, Jagjaguwar [Single].

Young, R. (2010), *Electric Eden: Unearthing Britain's Visionary Music*, Faber and Faber, London.

Young, R. (2013), 'The Blood on Satan's Claw Review', Uncut. Source: https://www.uncut.co.uk/reviews/dvd/blood-on-satans-claw Accessed 09/09/2018.

Chapter 2

EcoGothic Secrets: Venturing Beneath the Deep Dark Forest

Elizabeth Parker

When we think about 'the forest', we tend to think in extremes. We imagine this simultaneously real and fantastical space as either wholly 'good' or wholly 'bad'. When it is 'good', it is a remedial setting of light, wonder, and magic … and when it is 'bad', it is a dark, dangerous and terrifying wilderness. It is either – or, indeed, it is both – on the one side, the Enchanted Forest; on the other, the Gothic Forest. My concern, of course, in a collection focused on denizens of the *dark* woods, is with the latter: with the eerie underbelly of this sylvan environment.

The Gothic Forest is a widely recognised symbolic archetype in the Western imagination. As a site of trial, trepidation and terror, it is one of the most persistent and pervasive images in our fictions. From the demon-infested woods in *Gilgamesh* and the suicide forest of Dante, to the Forbidden Forest of the *Harry Potter* series (1997–2007) and the contemporary wealth of horror set in the woods, from *American Horror Story* (2011–present) to *The Ritual* (2017), we encounter this important cultural signifier again and again. The forest has always been a mainstay of the Gothic – as common, though less remarked on, as the graveyard, the castle and the abbey – and in recent years has become increasingly prevalent in popular culture. The freaky arboreal has proven highly saleable in the twenty-first century. In tandem with the deluge of more openly 'adult' retellings of fairy tales*, the Deep Dark Woods have featured across a variety of formats and genres, from YA fiction (*Pretty Little Liars* (2010–2017)) and crime dramas (*Hannibal* (2013–15)) to 'Nordic noir' (*Forbrydelsen* (2007–2012)) and everyday advertisements (Green & Blacks (2017)). The screen 'classics' that come to mind when we think of horror and the forest – such as *The Blair Witch Project* (1999), *The Evil Dead* (1981), and *Twin Peaks* (1990–1991) – have in recent years all been remade and revamped in various formats. A cultural awareness of the chilling appeal and market value of forested terrain is evidenced in such explicit titles as *The Forest* (2016), *The Woods* (2006) and *The Cabin in the Woods* (2012), which

---

* It is worthy of note that a significant number of our most popular and anthologised fairy tales in the West are set in the forest ('Little Red Riding Hood', 'Hansel and Gretel', 'Goldilocks and the Three Bears', 'Rapunzel', etc.) and that the parallels between fairy tales and horror texts are well documented (see, for example, Walter Rankin's *Grimm Pictures*, 2007).

transparently capitalise on our associations with the forested landscape to draw their audiences. It is starkly clear that though our forests in reality may be in frightening decline, the forests of our mind are not going anywhere.

It is not in doubt that the Gothic forest is continually and increasingly felt in the contemporary imagination; what *is* in doubt is exactly why. Though the 'Deep Dark Forest' is, as human geographer Yi-fu Tuan (1979, p. 1) remarks, a classic 'landscape of fear', for most of us there is little logical reason to fear it. We do not, usually, encounter it in our everyday lives and when we do, it has often already been recorded somewhere in minute cartographical detail. Meanwhile, it is common knowledge that the forest's larger predators are rare, extinct, or wholly fictitious. In short: statistically, as a twenty-first century human, it is extremely unlikely that you will be lost or eaten in the woods. And yet, as Sarah Maitland (2012, p. 200) attests, inside each of us 'post-enlightenment and would-be rational adults', there is still 'a child who is terrified by the wild wood'.

Our relationship to the forest environment is complex indeed. As Jay Appleton (1996, p. 29) notes, we have evolved as a species from 'forest-dwellers' to 'apartment-house dwellers': a transition which continues to be met with extreme ambivalence. On the one hand, there is the myth of progress, as we see ourselves evolved out of and beyond the densely wooded, uncultivated past; in the woods we were primitive, so this landscape threatens regression. On the other hand, however, forests symbolise nature untouched; in the woods we were pure, so this landscape promises redemption. Both scenarios are marked by fear: if the forest is not automatically terrifying, then it is something precious, which we have tragically largely *lost*. We are uncomfortable with entering a space that is now so alien and therefore frightening, *and* we are uncomfortable with the very fact that this space is now unknown.

It is my contention that the current prevalence of Gothic forests in popular culture is due in part to a widespread consensus that we are politically, spiritually and environmentally lost: humankind, as the aphorism goes, is collectively *in the woods*. The forest provides us with suitably complicated and contradictory symbolism, which expresses both a sense of panicked bewilderment* at being 'in the woods' in the first place, as well as a sense of some bygone simpler time, in which we were connected to a more 'natural' environment. Our seemingly endless texts that repeatedly place and endanger our characters in literal forests provide us, as horror is wont to do, not only with literalised manifestations of our fears, but with fantasies of escape: ordinarily with at least one cathartic example of a human surviving and exiting the woods, with a metonymic instance of us being 'out of the woods'.

---

*   The words 'panic' and 'bewilder' are both etymologically associated with the forest, with their roots relating to, respectively, the mischievous god Pan and the wilderness.

Interestingly, though our Gothic forests are frequently populated with a multifarious host of monstrous entities, there is the continual sense that what is truly frightening is not simply what is *in* the woods, but, as one character in *The Evil Dead* famously remarks, '*the woods themselves*'. This expression, 'the woods themselves', which seems straightforward enough, is deceptively simple. What exactly constitutes 'the forest' (the number of trees? the sounds? the ecosystems? etc.), let alone the exact source of its terrors, is open to debate. Indeed, Arthur Machen was on to something in *The Great God Pan* (1890) when he portentously described but never revealed 'that awful *secret* of the wood' [my emphasis], keenly aware that this setting's terror stems precisely from its own uncertainty.

In the current climate of anthropogenic environmental crisis, it is becoming progressively clear that we must endeavour to question and understand our increasingly uncertain relationship to the nonhuman world – and in particular, what makes us fear it (Hillard, 2009). The recent field of the ecoGothic, which, as its title suggests, brings together ecocriticism with Gothic studies, seeks to do just this. It sets out, as Simon C. Estok (2009, p. 685) asserts, to examine and 'theorise' human 'ecophobia' (our fears of the nonhuman). Interrogating our fears of the forest, of course, a landscape which once upon a time covered most of the Earth (Harrison, 1992, p. ix), is an important facet of this discussion. Moreover, it is our stories, and in particular our Gothic and horror stories, as Andrew Smith and William Hughes (2013) assert, that are best situated to capture and express our environmental anxieties – and so it is that our *representations* of the forest, the darker the better, demand deconstruction. This essay, through a discussion of several contemporary examples of Gothic forests in popular culture, examines how this idea of secrecy as to what exactly *lies beneath* this common, vague arboreal dread is manifested and expressed in our fictions – interrogating our ecoGothic secrets of the wood.

Referring portentously to the so-called 'horror' of the woods, but without ever actually stating or defining what in fact this horror exactly *is*, is quite common practice in texts which feature the Gothic forest. There is a common though often undiscussed tendency to talk about our fears of this landscape in decidedly *vague* terms. In the countless narratives which use the forest as a 'landscape of fear', to borrow Tuan's phrase, we repeatedly find a sense of imprecision and secrecy in the language used to describe the woods. For example, in *The Evil Dead* we are told 'there's *something* in the woods'; in *Hotel* it is said that '*something* terrible is happening out there'; in *The Ceremonies* we learn 'there are *things* in the trees'; in *Twin Peaks* we are warned that 'there's a *sort of* evil in the woods'; and in 'The Man Whom the Trees Loved' it is aptly announced that 'this tree and forest business is so vague and horrible!' Time and again we are given stern admonitions against entering this setting – for example, in *The Wizard of Oz*, the sign to the Haunted Forest reads 'I'd turn back if I were you' and in the film *The Woods* we are unequivocally told *'don't ever, ever go into the woods'* – but these admonitions are usually accompanied by very little, if any explanation. As summarised by one character in the 2013 film *Jug Face*: 'there's some weird shit going on in the woods', which – if we know what is good for us – 'we don't want anything to do with'. There is the presiding sense that the forest's 'awful secret', whatever it may be, is something that we *should not learn*.

This idea that the forest conceals some 'awful secret' is prevalent in many of our texts which are set in the Deep Dark Woods. This ambiguous and indeterminate secret usually serves to provide and underline a pervasive sense of ambient dread throughout the narrative. Though often it is merely hinted at and alluded to, this secret is sometimes made *physically manifest* in our stories, even if it is never seen. One such way in which this secret manifests – with remarkable frequency, I might add – is as something monstrous which lies hidden and buried *beneath* the forest's surface. In other words, our vague fears about *what lies beneath* our fears of the woods take on a rather literal form as *subterranean* terrors.

These buried monstrosities are, for the most part, unseen, but it is the threat of their revelation – much in line with Friedrich Schelling's (Freud, 1933, p. 130) definition of the uncanny as 'something which *ought* to have remained *secret and hidden*, but has come to light' – that effectively haunts these texts. The increasing prevalence of this trope of subterranean forest horror is demonstrative of a growing need to explain – and perhaps justify – widespread ecophobia. After all, the textbook reasons why we fear the wilderness – it is wild, uncontrollable and generally dwarfs human significance – have substantially motivated humankind's negative impact on non-human nature for thousands of years. In a time when we are unprecedentedly aware of our conduct in ecological crisis, it makes sense that we are interested – consciously and/or subconsciously – in what belies ecophobia. These texts which present us with images of, or allusions to something terrifying *beneath* the forest provide us with ways of working through something we don't quite understand. We can play with different versions of 'the woods' and different versions of ourselves within them. Schooled as we are in our various fairy tales, we expect the forest, as Richard Hayman (2003, p. 106) puts it, to serve as some sort of 'moral arbiter': it is a landscape of trial we must successfully traverse. Once we're in it, it is a space that will, as the scarecrow wisely warns us in *The Wizard of Oz* (1939), 'get darker before it gets lighter'. Like Little Red Riding Hood and Hansel and Gretel, though far from the path and dangerously lost, we must seek to find ourselves again.

We have many examples, in both literature and film, of texts that play with this idea that there is something terrible beneath the forest: so many, in fact, that we can begin to divide the *ways* in which these subterranean horrors take form. One standard example, for instance, of subterranean nasties in the forest manifests in the idea that this is an environment in which *bodies* are buried. Though some may think of wiccan ceremonies and green funerals, ordinarily, in the popular imagination, the forest is deemed a *wrongful* site of burial. It is often associated not with those who have died naturally or peacefully, but with those who have been murdered. It is a place of *un*rest for the dead.

In reality, this is seen in the frequent news stories which tell of bodies buried in the woods – a phenomenon that is sensationally underlined in documentaries such as *Cropsey* (2009) and the podcast *Serial* (2014–present). The former dwells on the woods of Staten Island as a near-natural 'home' for its titular protagonist: Cropsey, who is presented as a crazed murderer living in the wild. It slowly pans the ground of the forest, relaying the numbers of dead children found buried and often grotesquely posed in the woods – and hints strongly at multitudes of undiscovered corpses hidden beneath the surface. Its makers deliberately exploit and enhance the mythology around the nicknamed Cropsey figure: casting him as the Big Bad Monster living in the Big Bad Woods. Similarly, *Serial* relishes its portrayal of human bodies hidden in the woods. In one particularly haunting episode of this investigative podcast, which centres on an unsolved murder in Baltimore, we are introduced to the forest of Leakin Park. We learn that this space is hugely popular with criminals for hiding things and people out of sight. The episode, which notably takes its name after the forest, features an interview with a local resident who claims that there is a well-known saying about Leakin Park: you can't bury a body in these woods without discovering another. It is easy to see, with real life stories and subsequent legends such as these, how the forest setting in *itself* becomes the thing to be feared, when one imagines a whole host of cadavers hidden underfoot. Alexander Porteous in *Forests in Folklore and Mythology* (2012) discusses several more established and embellished legends from around the world in which the bodies of those buried in the forest *move* around the soil at night, disturbing the earth to walk through the woods, with only their heads above the ground.

We of course find examples in our literature and film which also show the woods as a site of unrest for the dead. Nathaniel Hawthorne's 'Roger Malvin's Burial' (1832) is a more well-known example of a Gothic story in which dying and remaining in the woods is shown as something to be feared indeed. In this tale, a young man is walking with his future father-in-law, Roger Malvin, in the wilderness. Malvin, it transpires, is dying and so the protagonist abandons him, with the promise of returning to take his body to be 'rightfully' buried amidst civilisation and his own people. The promise is broken and the young man is haunted by the 'wrongful' death in the forest which he has not 'corrected'. He is ultimately punished as an older man when he accidentally kills his own son on the exact site of Malvin's death.

There are various examples of the forest depicted as an unholy site for burial and one especially interesting recent example is Jim Mickle's artsy cannibal film *We Are What We Are* (2013), which centres on a family who live at the edge of a forest. The film is laden with clues as to some awful secret hidden beneath the surface. This subterranean secret manifests first in the prisoners kept beneath the family home, but ultimately in the woodland graves that hide the remains of the eaten victims, which are ultimately exposed in a flood. Indeed, the idea of something terrible concealed beneath ground level in a manmade dwelling is a staple of both horror and Gothic texts. In woodland as well as city dwellings in our fictions, we recognise basements as established sites of terror. In titles such as *The Blair Witch Project*, *The Evil Dead*, *The Cabin in the Woods*, and *The Woman*, it is the basement or the cellar *beneath* the woodland dwelling in which the darkest events unfold, or from which the darkness is released (see, for example, the *Necronomicon* in *Evil Dead* or the fateful objects in the basement of *The Cabin in the Woods*).

Most interestingly, subterranean woodland horrors commonly manifest in the form of *pits* and *holes* in the forest floor: visible entry- and exit-ways to and from whatever it is that lies beneath. These strange and often ostensibly harmless apertures are continually evocative of the forest's 'secret' – and of the idea that there is 'something hidden' which threatens to come to light. The increasing multitude of texts which feature these pits and holes play interestingly with the vague and various threats of the Gothic forest, slipping between ideas of this environment as a discerningly timeless, disorienting, dangerous, or carnivorous space. They play, too, with audiences' expectations of suspense and revelation, usually maintaining a firm sense of mystery and only sometimes showing us a physical monster.

The woods, as I have mentioned, are a place where we fear we will be eaten, be it by wild animals, anthropophagists, or witches and wendigos. The appearance in the forest floor of pits and holes is significant in this context because they emphasise the idea of the forest *itself* as a consuming threat, as these woodland orifices symbolise voracious *mouths* in the landscape, waiting to be fed. This idea of 'the woods themselves' threatening to 'eat' or 'swallow' those in its midst is one thematically explored in various tales of arboreal horror: from Algernon Blackwood's infamous story of *The Willows* (1907) (in which the eponymous trees close in, threatening to collectively swallow the victims) and his lesser known 'The Transfer' (1912) (which sees a mysterious pit at the edge of the woods consume the energy of its victims above), to arthouse horror flicks like the surrealist classic *Little Otík* (2000) (which features a particularly disturbing stop-animation creature of insatiable arboreal monstrosity) and recent bestsellers like Naomi Novik's *Uprooted* (2015) (in which 'heart trees' consume, embalm and amalgamate with humans).

The appearance of forest 'mouths', which open to something terrifying below, is also indicative of the recurrent image of *hell* beneath the woods. We might think, in terms of linguistic association, of 'the mouth of hell', or the fact that hell is referred to as a 'pit' at various points in the Bible. We may think, too, of Dante's suicide forest in the seventh circle of hell. Indeed, the idea that hell itself resides beneath the surface of the forest is recurrent in the Western cultural imagination. This is due in part to the fact that we commonly regard the forest as an 'anti-Christian' space (Adam and Eve were cast out of the cultivated garden into the unwanted wilderness, or 'Satan's church', as it is termed in Lars von Trier's *Antichrist*) and to the commonly held idea that hell is always physically *beneath* us, drawing us ever downwards to damnation.

Several texts illustrate these ideas. In David Lynch's cult classic *Twin Peaks*, the forest is of enormous – if consistently vague – significance throughout. It is alluded to visually, thematically and explicitly, yet its seductions and its threats remain uncertain. Early on, we are told merely that there is 'something very, very strange in these old woods' and we are encouraged, increasingly, to somehow link the forest with the mysterious murder of Laura Palmer, which lies at the centre of the show. It ultimately transpires that this murder's explanation, in part, lies *beneath* the surrounding woods of Twin Peaks. We learn eventually that three distinct realms exist beneath the trees – The White Lodge, The Black Lodge, and the Red Room – each of which, respectively, embodies our ideas about the woods as idyllic, as monstrous and as purgatorial.

Focusing on the two extremes, The White Lodge – described as a place of 'great goodness' and saccharine excess' – is a clear embodiment of the Enchanted Forest, whilst The Black Lodge – described as 'a place of darkness' and even as 'the evil in the woods of Twin Peaks' – is a clear embodiment of the *Gothic* forest. We do see inside the Red Room, the purgatorial space, but we are never shown the Black Lodge, the source of the 'evil in the woods', so its awful secrecy remains intact. We see only its entrance, which fittingly, takes the form of an ominous and metonymic pit in a small clearing in the woods. In the finale to the original series, we see our protagonist, Dale Cooper (Kyle MacLachlan), enter this pit and though he seems to emerge, we learn in the final shot that his authentic self has remained trapped beneath the woods in this version of hell and the thing taking his form in the world above is an imposter.

Interestingly, we are told of these mysterious spaces beneath the forest by Native American Deputy Hawk (Michael Horse), who is the most knowledgeable source on the dangers of the woods. His warnings against seeking out the Black Lodge mark this forested space as 'taboo Indian land' – a significant trope in American arboreal horror, indicative of the idea that America itself hides something dark beneath, as it is, as Michael Rogin (1991, p. 5) argues, built on 'Indian graves'. Chad Crawford Kinkle's fascinating film *Jug Face* features a pit which is visually remarkably similar to the entrance to the Black Lodge in *Twin Peaks*. Furthermore, this film also plays with the idea of 'taboo Indian land', as we learn that 'The Pit' – its so-named forest deity of sorts – marks a space in the woods that once upon a time was deeply feared and avoided by Native Americans. *Jug Face* centres on a small community dwelling in the depths of the Tennessee woods who worship this Pit as their God, ritualistically sacrificing their own members, which they *feed* to the Pit in accordance with its demands in return for good health. The voracious Pit, which turns red when fed, then slowly 'digests' the human sacrifice into its unseen abyss, again symbolically recalls the mouth of hell. Though we see the Pit again and again, along with the bloody effects of its whims and ire, we never actually *see* the exact horrors that it contains. At most, we see its muddy waters bloodied and have a POV shot hurtling through the woods when it hunts and kills those who endeavour to escape it, but its specificities remain disturbingly vague throughout.

Though in texts like *Twin Peaks* and *Jug Face*, we never see what lies beneath the woods inside its apertures, this is not always the case. In numerous examples, we have texts which dangle the vague threat of something hideous, buried or residing in a pit or hole beneath the woods, but choose to ultimately reveal it. For instance, in Richard Layman's *The Woods Are Dark*, it transpires that the central horror of the forest stems from a huge, tentacled, bloodthirsty monster, which resides in a deep pit in the woods, waiting – much like The Pit in *Jug Face* – to be ritualistically fed. This novel ends in chaos, with the monster emerging from the depths of the forest, with little hope for its extermination.

T.E.D. Klein's masterclass in Weird fiction, *The Ceremonies*, similarly reveals its monster in its final moments. Klein was an enormous fan of Arthur Machen – the man who penned the line 'that awful secret of the wood' – and his 1984 novel serves not only as an homage to Machen, but to the 'awful secret' that he frequently proffered, but never quite revealed. In his 500-page tome, Klein's forest is an ambient threat throughout, but the literally underlying source of its terror is discovered only on the very last page. We are made increasingly aware, however, throughout the text, that there is *something* horrible concealed in the woods.

The novel's main adversary, a man named Rosebottom, seeks to awaken a mysterious, evil force in the woods through the performance of multiple and increasingly sinister ceremonies. As he slowly progresses in his task, a huge mound of earth rises inexplicably in the forest, in a clearing known as 'McKinney's Neck' (which in fact is another example of 'taboo Indian land' and – with its etymology meaning 'place of burning' – a further allusion to this idea of arboreal hell). The mound is an inversion of the pit or hole, as here what lies beneath is not buried beneath the surface, but threatens to come free as it pushes up out of the earth. The mound in itself is not obviously dangerous, but its presence portentously haunts the text throughout. In the end, the unseen danger beneath this forest is *not* released, and Rosie is defeated, but on the final page, we are left with a surreal and terrifying glimpse of what *could* have been released from beneath the forest: a colossal, monstrous behemoth, of planetary proportions. This monster exists beneath *all* of human civilisation, but significantly could only have been awoken and could only have emerged from *beneath the forest*, as its horrors are interestingly and inextricably bound to this environment.

In contemporary popular culture we also have examples of literally monstrous subterranean forest threats. In *Stranger Things* (2016–present), for example, we have the demogorgons and the Shadow Monster from the Upside Down: a parallel universe that can significantly be accessed by portals in the woods, which take the form of holes in the bases of trees in the woods, which visually seem to swallow those who force their ways in. Indeed, there seems a tendency in recent years with titles such as *Jordskott* and *Dark* to point to the existence of entire *worlds* beneath the forest, threatening to impinge upon our own – and interestingly in both instances holes or pits in the forest floor are of portentous significance (in the former, growing sinkholes threaten the stability of settled locals and in the latter, literally explosive matter is precariously hidden in pits in the woods).

It is well-established that the monster, usually, serves as some reflection of the human. The 'other', time and again, is a mere projection of the 'self'. It is fitting, then, that as we explore subterranean forest monstrosities, we are indirectly exploring superterranean human monstrosities. Indeed, the texts which seem to make the most critical impact and have the most longevity tend to be those which exploit and test the tension between the human and the inhuman and leave us uncertain, at least for the majority of the work, as to whether we are dealing with the supernatural or the mundane. Several texts in recent years are explicitly conscious of this ostensible dichotomy.

Lucile Had ihaliloviæ's film *Innocence* (2004) exposes one of the forest's most infamous predators, The Big Bad Wolf, as fully human, returning to Perrault's rendition of 'Little Red Riding Hood', which explicitly warns against the temptations of seductive males, for inspiration. The film, which centres on a largely adult-less seeming utopia of children in the forest, plays repeatedly with our associations with the woods, fairy tales, and endangered children. Significantly, it ominously alludes throughout to the mystery of what is *beneath* the woods, as the children routinely descend beneath the surface. Eventually, we discover that they are entering an underground theatre, replete with voyeuristic adult males, who access the theatre via a secret underground train. We learn that it is these men, these 'big bad wolves', paying to see the little girls, or 'little reds' who fund the eerie idyll. What lies beneath the threat of the woods, here, is the threat of urban and rapacious humanity.

M. Night Shyamalan's *The Village* (2004) similarly plays with our cultural associations with 'Little Red Riding Hood', here inverting them as in this film our substitute for Little Red wears yellow, whilst it is the monsters of the woods who are adorned in red capes. Shyamalan plays throughout with the question of if the monsters are 'real': we seem to discover that they are in fact the Elders of a community, dressed up in costumes, seeking to frighten the younger generations into remaining in this alternative woodland society. However, in the final act, it seems that we encounter the real thing on which the legends are based, but in a further twist we learn that this too is a human in disguise (though the blind protagonist does not know this and unwittingly kills her ostensible adversary). Significantly, the man dressed as the monster is killed by falling into a trap in the woods: into a literal pit in the forest's floor. The protagonist cannot see into the pit; she sees only the monster in her mind, but the audience is shown that what truly resides beneath the surface is a human disguised.

This level of meta-consciousness about various woodland subterranean nasties arguably reaches its apex in Drew Goddard and Joss Whedon's *The Cabin in the Woods*. The premise in this film is that once a year, secret, but elaborate and expansive organisations across the world cultivate real-life horror film scenarios in which unknowing victims are killed in order to appease ancient gods, thus allowing for the continuation of human existence as we know it (a sort of mass-scale version of the covenants we see in *Jug Face* and *The Woods Are Dark* (1981)). The action of the film centres on the American entry, which – as the title explicitly suggests – takes place in the clichéd setting of the cabin in the woods (the '*the*' in the title drawing attention to the archetypal nature of this setting). The horrors that unfold in this environment are monitored and largely orchestrated by a huge corporate organisation, known as 'The Complex', who are situated literally beneath the woods in question. They hold a plethora of incarcerated and neatly organised fantastical monsters, which are individually released only in consequence to the so-called 'transgressions' made by the victims above. When the monsters successfully slay their prey, the victims' blood trickles down through the earth, *beneath* the forest, to eventually reach the mysterious, unseen and voracious entities known only as 'The Ancient Ones'.

We are presented here with an intriguingly explicit and unusually complicated manifestation of this idea that *something* sinister underlies the forest in this conscious meta-interrogation into the workings and motivations of horror as a genre and, more specifically, of horror *in the woods*. The promotional image for the film, which presents the cabin in the style of a Rubik's Cube, immediately draws attention to examining it from all sides – even and especially from underneath. Meanwhile, the film itself ultimately presents us with various revelations of a complex subterranean structure. On the surface, we have the forest and the cabin itself; directly beneath this, we have The Complex; beneath *this*, we have what Katherine A. Wagner (2013, p. 1) has called 'the warren of monsters' and beneath *this*, at the very deepest level, we have The Ancient Ones.

The film plays intelligently with our fears of both human *and* nonhuman monsters in the forest. Seemingly, it is the 'real' monsters that are to be feared the most, as they blindly and animalistically destroy, whilst those in The Complex, ostensibly, are under a sort of necessary duress, 'killing only a few for the good of the many'. The film's twist comes at the very end, when the sacrificial ritual is ultimately unsuccessful, and the Ancient Ones, unappeased, break loose: quite literally releasing hell on Earth. Once again, we have this symbol of hell *beneath* the forest, threatening to surface. In the very final image we see a colossal hand, belonging to one of the Ancient Ones, burst out from beneath the forest, destroying the cabin and everything around it. What is so significant about this image is the fact that the hand is clearly *human*: the mysterious 'gods', or Ancient Ones, are none other than *us*. The motivations for the violence we have seen, therefore, are not divinely decreed. The bloodlust, ultimately, is entirely our own, as both consumers of horror and as *humans*, and it is this truth – or 'awful secret' – that is here eventually revealed.

It is surprising, given the frequency with which subterranean forest horrors exist in our fictions, how little this phenomenon is discussed. The archetypal Gothic forest remains as popular a 'landscape of fear' as ever and arguably is increasing in its prevalence. In the current climate of the ever-present threat of ecological disaster, our relationship to the non-human or more-than-human world comes increasingly under scrutiny. In a time when we are very much metaphorically 'in the woods', but in reality grow increasingly distant from this landscape as we lose millions of acres of woodland yearly through deforestation, the need for understanding is acute. The ecoGothic intention to interrogate ecophobia is pertinent indeed – not merely in terms of its existence, but as much in terms of its absence.

What seems to have happened is that ecophobia has in the past justified the mass-subjugation of nature, but has now been in part displaced by an *indifference* to nature, which is every bit, if not more dangerous. We have, as Robert Pogue Harrison (1992, p. 121) argues, lost the ability to see the forest as 'strange, monstrous, and enchanting'. His central use of the word 'monstrous' here is interesting: almost as though it is a consequence of strangeness and a requisite of enchantment. Indeed, it is my contention that what we need now is a 'positive ecophobia' of sorts: a reawakening to the mysteries and darknesses of nature, but with the outcome of fear and respect, as opposed to fear and destruction. We are using fiction to immerse ourselves in forests of the mind as we lose forests of the land. In these imagined landscapes, we work *through* something and in these texts that feature subterranean monstrosities, we look beneath the surface, questioning our relationship to fear and nature. Though the exploration of what belies our nightmares of the wilderness, we can valuably reengage with the awesomeness of nature.

References

Appleton, J. (1996). *The Experience of Landscape,* Chichester: John Wiley and Sons.

Blackwood, A. (1907, 2005). *The Willows*, USA: Wildside Press.

_____ (1912). *Pan's Garden: A Volume of Nature Stories,* London: Macmillan and Co.

Estok, S. C. (2009). 'Theorising in a Space of Ambivalent Openness: Ecocriticism and Ecophobia', *Interdisciplinary Studies in Literature and the Environment (ISLE)*, 16(2), 203–225.

Freud, S. (2003). *The Uncanny*, translated by Phillips, A. and McLintock, D., London: Penguin Books.

Harrison, R. (1992). *Forests: The Shadow of Civilisation,* Chicago: Chicago University Press.

Hayman, R. (2003). *Trees, Woodland and Civilisation*, London: Palgrave Macmillan.

Hillard, T. J. (2009). '"Deep Into the Darkness Peering": An Essay on Gothic Nature', *Interdisciplinary Studies in Literature and the Environment (ISLE)*, 16(4), 685–695.

Machen, A. (2006). *Tales of Horror and the Supernatural,* Leyburn: Tartarus Press.

Maitland, S. (2012). *Gossip from the Forest: The Tangled Roots of our Forests and Fairy Tales*, London: Granta Books.

Mitchell, S. ed. (2004). *Gilgamesh*, translated by Mitchell, S., London: Profile Books.

Novik, N. (2015). *Uprooted*, Oxford: Macmillan.

Porteous, A. (2012). *The Forest in Folklore and Mythology,* New York: Macmillan.

Smith, A. and Hughes, W. ed. (2013). *EcoGothic,* Manchester: Manchester University Press.

Rankin, W. (2007). *Grimm Pictures: Fairy Tale Archetypes in Eight Horror and Suspense Films,* North Carolina: McFarland and Co.

Rogin, M. (1991). *Fathers and Children: Andrew Jackson and the Subjugation of the Indian,* New Jersey: Transaction Publishers.

Shyamalan, M. N. (2004). *The Village [DVD]*, United States: Touchstone Pictures.

This American life (2014) 'Serial' [podcast]. www.serialpodcast.com [accessed 15th Jul 2016].

Tuan, Y. (1979). *Landscapes of Fear*, Oxford: Basil Blackwell.

Wagner, K. (2013). 'Haven't We Been Here Before?: The Cabin in the Woods, the Horror Genre, and Placelessness', Slayage: The Journal of joss Whedon Studies Association, 10(2).

Filmography

Cropsey (2009). *[DVD]* United States: Breaking Glass Pictures.

Hotel (2004). [DVD] Austria: Coop99.

Innocence (2004). [DVD] France: Artificial Eye.

Jug Face (2013). [DVD] United States: Modernciné.

Little Otík (2000). [DVD] Czech Republic: Zeitgeist Films.

Stranger Things (2016–present). [DVD] USA: Netflix.

The Blair Witch Project (2003). [DVD] USA: 20th Century Fox.

The Cabin in the Woods (2012). [DVD] United States: Mutant Enemy Productions.

The Evil Dead (2013). *[DVD] United States:* TriStar Pictures.

The Wizard of Oz (1939). [DVD] United States: Metro-Goldwyn-Meyer.

The Woman (2011). [DVD] United States: Modernciné.

Twin Peaks (1990–1). [DVD] United States: Lynch/Frost Productions.

We Are What We Are (2013). [DVD] United States: Entertainment One.

Chapter 3

Holy monstrosity of arborescence in Brian Catling's *The Vorrh*

András Fodor

Introduction

The woods depicted in Brian Catling's debut *The Vorrh* represent a forbidden and sacred location that shatters the shared quotidian sense of time and space. Both of these features of conventional reality are devoured by this 'mother of forests' (Catling, 2016, p. 34) as the author describes it. Reality as such has to be 'potentially constructed by the subjects who inhabit it' (García, 2015, p. 1), otherwise the cosmos falls prey to chaos as Patricia García points out. Therefore, any recollection or reconstruction of positionality within the site of Vorrh proves to be next to impossible for the characters. Memories of time spent in it cannot be recalled; this contained chaos overrules the reality. In the narrative, many characters visit this jungle-like forest for different purposes, either to accomplish their Western and colonial urge to locate 'all the countries of the world in a single spatial frame' (García, 2015, p. 81) as Peter Williams does, who suffers from multiple personality disorder owing to the influence of the woods; or to overcome their Otherness by the power and knowledge of the denizens of the Vorrh, like the cyclops does, Ishmael who was raised by 'the Kin ... [those] gentle, dark-brown machines that ... looked like him in shape but were made from different material' (Catling, 2016, p. 33). On the one hand, in the case of Peter Williams who becomes Oneofthewilliams, the chosen one, the messiah for the natives, the Vorrh turns the colonizer–native divide topsy-turvy, and constructs an Other from the Westerner. On the other hand, in order to rectify Ishmael's condition of one-eyedness, he receives a second eye, after which he could join 'those who see [him] the wrong way' (Catling, 2016, p. 416) and return to the society of Essenwald.

Not only do these two point of view characters epitomise the dichotomy of holiness and monstrosity of the narrative space, a concept of Marie-Laure Ryan that is 'the physically existing environment in which characters live and move', but also the settings, defined too by Ryan as 'the general socio-historico-geographical environment in which the action takes place', are fathomed in this particular dyad in this chapter (Ryan, 1991, p. 3). The Vorrh and the city of Essenwald maintain a very close relationship with each other, an almost symbiotic one. The main aim of this chapter is to investigate this interrelation via the methods of spatiality from the vantage point of world-building and from the aspect of two protagonists whose ontological and epistemological metamorphoses, I argue, are assigned to the Vorrh itself. This transfiguration is connected to colonialism as well. But capturing the uncertainties ascribed to the space of the forest, the chapter hinges on Patricia García's reading of fantastical spaces and partly on Michel Foucault's understanding of heterotopia.

Furthermore, in order to perceive and scrutinize the heterogenity of the space in its complexity, I also pivot on the idea of Gilles Deleuze's any-space-whatever. Albeit this Deleuzian term is connected to cinema, Sarah K. Cantrell points out in her essay, '"I solemnly swear I am up to no good": Foucault's Heterotopias and Deleuze's Any-Spaces-Whatever in J. K. Rowling's Harry Potter Series' that any-space-whatever as a concept 'possesses an unlimited potential for transformation and reconfiguration' (Cantrell, 2011, p. 205) and '[G]iven the lack of definitive, unifying relationships between its multiple parts, the any-space-whatever is a space of infinite assembly and combination' (Cantrell, 2011, p. 205), thus, pertinent to other sorts of narratives as well.

Additionally, Cantrell calls attention to the difference between the irreconcilable features of the heterotopia and any-space-whatever that 'heterotopias remain separate from the places that surround them, the any-space-whatever possesses the capacity to metamorphose into any number of potential and contradictory spaces' (2011, p. 205). However, I postulate that this differentiation is problematic in *The Vorrh* neither on the level of settings and narrative spaces, nor on the level of point of view characters. So the paper puts forward the understanding of the Vorrh as an any-space-whatever to the city and Essenwald as a heterotopia to the forest. On the level of point of view characters, Ishmael goes through so many transformations so he can be understood as somebody who has the features of any-space-whatever, whereas Peter Williams can be interpreted as he is endowed with certain heterotopian features. Both Deleuze's and Foucault's concepts conduce to the comprehension of the notions of Fantastic of Space and Fantastic of Place that adhere to the perusal of Patricia García.

Theoretical background

In order to provide a theoretical framework for the paper, utterly different ideas have to be harmonized in it. Consequently, holiness and monstrosity have to be connected to the concepts of space and place; and to the native and the colonizer. However, the characters of Ishmael and Peter Williams are hybrids in the sense that they cannot be sharply defined, categorized along the lines of either/or; they belong to both classes of holy and monstrous. The paper proposes that these ideas have to be taken into consideration.

The opposition of holiness and monstrosity is understood from a Western perspective. These two ideas are to be comprehended as whether they are controllable by the colonizer. In this context holiness can only be part of the establishment, whereas the feature of monstrosity can only belong to the natives. The notion of place can be connected to a rule-bound logic; according to Patricia García, it is 'fundamentally tied to the articulation, or materialisation, of 'space' (García, 2015, p. 20). She argues in her book, *Space and the Postmodern Fantastic in Contemporary Literature: The Architectural Void* that place 'is a human invention, constricted by ritual markings that invest it with meaning and attach to it functions and values' and bears 'three characteristics: identity, relations ... and history' (García, 2015, p. 20).

In the case of Essenwald, its identity stems from and is validated by the city it copies from the colonizing Europe. Its relation to its surroundings can be described as exploitative and capitalist, since it 'fed on trees, [is] devouring the myriad of different species that ferociously grew there' (Catling, 2016, p. 35). The novel points out this parasitic act, by saying that all 'this appetite was allowed by the forest' (Catling, 2016, p. 35). Consequently, the space of the woods is powerful enough to control this relationship. Essenwald's history is also not without difficulties, since '[I]t was built over a century and a half, the core of its imitation now so old that it had become genuine' (Catling, 2016, p. 33). It lacks anything that can be deemed as simply historical.

The feature of monstrosity of the Vorrh surfaces as a condition of the space from the perspective of the Western perceiver by defying the colonizer's attempt to control it. Since this wilderness is observed as space, it lacks the three characteristics of places. To counterbalance this, Essenwald is the product of colonization, a logical, organized location with every aspect of place; thus, it is observed as ontologically and epistemologically known and familiar. It carries the quality of holiness in relation to the Vorrh. In the framework of colonization, the settlement overcomes its ordinariness and provides a much needed shelter, a church of culture for the Europeans.

The Vorrh meets the criteria of what Patricia García calls the Fantastic of Space, with reference to 'a literary phenomenon where the normal laws of physical space that rule our extratextual experience are not respected' (García, 2015, p. 26) and it functions as '*agent* of the transgression, provoking the breach of logical laws' (García, 2015, p. 33). Essenwald provides the reading of Fantastic of Place of itself by covering the existence of Ishmael, a cyclops of enigmatic origin. Because of that it becomes 'the *host* of the fantastic agent' (García, 2015, p. 33).

The city of Essenwald as place and its heterotopian nature towards the Vorrh

The idea of the city of Essenwald (the name of the city comes from German, from the words for 'to eat' and 'forest') has to be problematised in order to fathom the concepts of space and place within the context of Catling's novel. From the perspective of the reader, it is assumed that Essenwald appears to be a place with its organized life, ontologically and epistemologically comprehensible conduct of living. It is introduced as being prosperous, busy and full of movement, with solid roads and train lines scrolling out from its [Essenwald's] frantic, lustrous heart' (Catling, 2016, p. 33). So there is an intelligible framework, known references in it for the reader. Whereas the Vorrh defies all of these conditions and it is suggested that it lacks everything that may provide a point of orientation. It is incomprehensible for the colonizer, it harbours monsters, the first man, Adam, who after '[e]ach century ... loses a skin of humanity, peeling back through the animals to dust' (Catling, 2016, p. 248). So it is still the fearful, unknown and untamed space that transforms the companions of Ulysses into swine as Bertrand Westphal puts it. Since it is the garden for God, those who enter the wilderness of Vorrh are not protected by any sort of deity in their venture; consequently, they are altered at the end of their journeys.

First of all, it should be noted that the story is set in Africa after the Great War. The reason why this should be highlighted is that the framework in which the story takes place stems from the epoch of colonization, where the opposition between the colonizer and the native cannot be overcome. In addition to this contrast the sexual territorialization should also just be briefly mentioned. Bertrand Westphal relying on ancient Greek literature, explains this metaphorization in which the explorers are males, who penetrate the Terra Incognita, the females. In Catling's novel, the Vorrh is seen as female, whereas the European colonizer as the male figure. On the level of characters, this distinctive feature can be found in Irrinipeste, the female seer of the natives, who dies and provides a weapon from her spine for the colonizer, Peter Williams to defend himself against the rage of Vorrh, the 'mother of forests' (Catling, 2016, p. 34). Her endeavour proves to be futile. However, in the novel the forest of Vorrh does not let itself be subjugated into the yoke of the British colonial power. But through the fantastical features of the woods, it can sabotage the attempts of the empire to pinpoint, to circumscribe and to define it into 'a single spatial frame' as Patricia García puts it (García, 2015, p. 81) as a mode to establish and force meaning on its yet unknown land.

Secondly, the relationship between the artifact city, Essenwald, and the natural area, the Vorrh, has to be established. The novel presents Essenwald as

> a European city, imported piece by piece to the Dark Continent and reassembled in a vast clearing made in the perimeter of the forest. It was built

over a century and a half, the core of its imitation now so old that it had become genuine, while the extremes of weather had set about another form of fakery, forcing the actions of seasons through the high velocity of tropical tantrum (Catling, 2016, p. 33).

It admits its non-genuine origin, that it is a duplicate of a city possibly on the map of Europe in order to aim to eliminate the distance between the unknown and the colonizer. Bertrand Westphal calls attention to the fact of the working method of the colonist in which one undertakes to construct a spatial hierarchy between the areas. The unknown, that cannot be named and put on a map, is frightening for the conqueror, thus, a 'mixture of violence and sexual ambiguity that created the zone of preliminary turbulence' provides the solution that a European man can employ (Westphal, 2016, p. 118).

The Vorrh is proposed as the 'mother of forests; [that it is] ancient beyond language, older than every known species' (Catling, 2016, p. 34). It is positioned partly as a mystery that has to be solved by the settlers and/or as an entity that 'mimicked Europe, smuggling a fake winter for a week or two, dropping temperatures and making the city look and feel like its progenitor' (Catling, 2016, p. 34). The latter feature reveals a peculiar familiarity for the denizens of Essenwald. Although Westphal argues that 'the European colonial powers that invested in overseas lands have strived to offer their citizens a reading grid to conquer space or spaces already conquered and "localized" – that is to say, spaces transformed into places wrapped in a reassuring onomastic' (Westphal, 2016, p. 130), this imitation is not strong enough to operate as a simulacrum of Europe.

In his book, *The Plausible World: A Geocritical Approach to Space, Place, and Maps*, Westphal relies on Giorgio Agamben's idea of the anthropological machine that 'aims to produce the human through a set of oppositions contrasting the human and the animal or the human and the inhuman. This machine carries a tautology, since the human, a quasi-divine figure, is always predetermined' (Westphal, 2016, p. 112). As Westphal explains, this practice

> is set in motion whenever the individual is confronted with a new space, which is confusing and which he must just as soon enclose. It helps him understand the area of ontological indeterminacy that arises before him. It helps him transform that which is dislocated (*dis-locatus*) into a controllable place (*locus*). It performs an integrative function. Brutally integrative. It immediately precedes the invention – that is, the transformation of an indefinable space into a common place (Westphal, 2016, p. 113).

Consequently, a power structure can be identified in this dyad whose purpose is 'to take position of a *place*, the *space* must be emptied of its spatiality' (Westphal, 2016, p. 126). Consequently, it means the incorporation of the Vorrh on the map. The main issue with the forest is that it is devoid of anything that is ontologically and epistemologically comprehensible for the colonists. It can 'devour a thousand of their [humans'] little lives in a microsecond of their uninterrupted, unfathomable time. So vast was its acreage, it also made its demands of time, splitting the toiling sun into zones outside of normal calibration' (Catling, 2016, p. 34). However, the anthropological machine fails to transform the space of Vorrh into the place of the forest. It would lose its condition of being named Vorrh, because the colonizer had it renamed to something familiar. Therefore, Westphal points out that 'to "domesticate" otherness by a set of soothing metaphors' (Westphal, 2016, p. 130), which is a technique, cannot be employed; therefore, the possibility of losing and 'dissolving into an uncontrollable animality' as the colonizer enters the Vorrh is very likely (Westphal, 2016, p. 120).

Thirdly, Essenwald as a place, a centre of culture and civilization, provides a haven for an Other, a cyclops. But according to the power structure, Ishmael should be understood as a someone whose origin could have been found in the Vorrh. Contrary to that expectation, the power of the colonizer fails to provide help for his condition of having only one eye; consequently, he decides to escape from the city and obtains another eye in the forest, which also confirms the failure of the anthropological machine project. He leaves as an Other and returns as a non-Other, tamed, Western man with a pair of eyes.

Even though Essenwald is perceived as a place from the standpoint of colonists, from the point of view of the Vorrh, it is simply a heterotopia 'because all of the Vorrh is sacred, from its outer rings into its core. The time and the space are an intrusion: all will offend' (Catling, p. 189). Two of the reality-constructing principles with which the European man is able to manage and control its surrounding problematize the purpose of Essenwald's existence. Michel Foucault in his essay 'Of Other Spaces' specifies that heterotopias 'are most often linked to slices in time' (Foucault, 1986, p. 26). Therefore, the story of a native in which this person narrates to a Westerner that

> Essenwald is a library to the forest, an appendage. It was attracted here when the Vorrh was already ancient. The physical closeness of so many people gives God a direct index to the current ways of mankind; his angels can learn there. It is an open shelf (Catling, 2016, p. 189),

is one that illustrates the heterotopian features of Essenwald.

The Vorrh as space and any-space-whatever to Essenwald

Approaching the processes of the holy and monstrous metamorphoses that take place in the Vorrh, the forest itself has to be considered first from the perspective of spatiality. The Vorrh as an area condenses the feature of space within itself and hampers the understanding of consensual time and space.

Catling writes that the woods 'made its demands of time, splitting the toiling sun into zones outside of normal calibration; a theoretical traveller, passing through its entire breadth on foot, would have to stop at its centre and wait at least a week for his soul to catch up' (Catling, 2016, p. 34). According to one of the characters, 'No son of Adam is allowed [into the Vorrh], for God walks there' (Catling, 2016, p. 55), who thinks 'in wordly ways' and 'wears a gown of senses, woven in our [characters'] time' (Catling, 2016, p. 56).

The Vorrh as an infamous location in the novel also has to be scrutinized. There are characters who go into this unknown wilderness. The pair of them, one, a Frenchman, who can be understood as he belongs to the colonizing power, the other one a native, aim to 'traverse the entire forest' (Catling, 2016, p. 55). This chapter understands this as a colonizing attempt to construct place from space. The Vorrh shares a feature that Bertrand Westphal describes as an 'area where the human condition slipped toward the nonhuman' (Westphal, 2016, p. 111), which can be comprehended as a condition of the forest that subverts and resists the authorial gaze of the colonist. Its refusal to be put down on a map as a 'spatial idea of the construction of a reality' (García, 2015, p. 82) illustrates that even the concept of space as such can be problematic in relation to it. Patricia García relies on Bertrand Westphal when she explains the two concepts of space and place:

> 'Place' is understood as framed space and 'space' as a wider entity constituted by the physical properties of its places and by the way in which these places relate to each other. Space is thus articulated and divided into places and, conversely, places are located in space (García, 2015, p. 20).

Furthermore, to specify these concepts, it should be underlined that space is 'conceived of as an abstract physical category composed of a set of relations and dimensions' (García, 2015, p. 21), whereas places 'are constricted by a set of frames that define their physical shape, render them mathematically measurable and allow them to be mapped or localised within a coordinate system' (García, 2015, p. 21). From the vantage point of dyad of heterotopia and any-space-whatever, Vorrh is considered to be the latter toward the settlement.

Deleuze describes any-space-whatever as a space that

> has merely lost its homogeneity, that is, the principle of its metric relations or the connection of its own parts, so that the linkages can be made in an infinite number of ways (Deleuze, 1986, p. 109).

From the standpoint of the colonist it is inconceivable to comprehend the Vorrh. Its potentiality lies in the situation in which its 'capacity to meta-morphose into any number of potential and contradictory spaces' can be actualised (Cantrell, 2011, p. 205). From the perspective of spatiality, the main issue is the relationship between Essenwald and Vorrh. The two locations differ from each entirely, but Vorrh still connects and knots them together into the narrative space. As space, it incorporates Essenwald as place and metamorphoses those who leave the settlement.

The Fantastic of Space and the Fantastic of Place

This disruption of space–time transforms space and place into Fantastic of Space and Fantastic of Place. Space is understood as open and by that it also means that it 'has no trodden paths and signposts. It has no fixed pattern of established human meaning' (Tuan, 1977, p. 54) as Yi-Fu Tuan argues in his book, *Space and Place: The Perspective of Experience*. Although Tuan advocates this non-fixity of human meaning as positive, in the context of the novel it is deemed it as rather problematic. Because of the freedom that the Vorrh employs as space, the wilderness looms over the place of Essenwald, the space of the forest metamorphoses then actualises the city as the Vorrh's heterotopian place. The supernatural feature of Vorrh stems from the impossibility of meaning-making as a precondition of controlled orientation.

The Western colonizers cannot construct an articulated space from the forest, place. The woods is devoid of closeness and, according to García, of place, which is 'fundamentally tied to the articulation'. She postulates that that notion 'is a human invention, constricted by ritual markings that invest it with meaning and attach to it functions and values' and bears 'three characteristics: identity, relations ... and history' (García, 2015, p. 20). The novel provides bits of information in relation to these above mentioned characteristics about the Vorrh, but all of them are too sublime in the sense that they cannot be fathomed by human beings.

The Fantastic of Space is seen by García as 'the *agent* of the transgression, provoking the breach of logical laws' (García, 2015, p. 33). From this perspective the Vorrh aims for this condition. It defies quotidian epistemological and ontological reality, though this denial not only affects the narrative space and the settings, but also influences the native characters in such a way as to transform them 'into other beings, beings devoid of purpose, identity, or meaning' (Catling, p. 35). They become die Verlorenen, the Limboia, who 'have been to the Vorrh too many times' (187). Essenwald is perceived as the Fantastic of Place, a concept by García in which 'space is seen as the *host* of the fantastic agent' (García, 2015, p. 33), since it harbours Ishmael, a cyclops of enigmatic origin whose condition is more akin to anything that comes from the Vorrh. Apart from him, there is nothing that infiltrates the shared reality on account of the Vorrh that has been domesticated into the narrative space.

The metamorphoses of Peter Williams and Ishmael

What the Vorrh does to Peter Williams is entirely different from what happened with Ishmael. The man is turned into Oneofthewilliams, a messiah figure to the natives, the True People. The Westerner arrives as a veteran of the Great War and starts to work as a trainer for the new police force. '[T]he outpost was to the southeast of the Vorrh, two hundred miles from the city and two thousand years away' (Catling, 2016, p. 17). He is called to an incident where he encounters a young woman, Irrinipeste, a seer of the natives. He finds 'a young woman knelt on the floor [of the church], surrounded by books, with one heavy foolscap tome open before her. She was naked and menstruating heavily'; she desecrates the holy place of the church (Catling, 2016, pp. 20–21). The events in the novel do not follow the chronological order, so right at the beginning of the novel she dies. The woman's spine becomes a sentient bow and as such, it is a representation of space and any-space-whatever. Putting it differently, it has a metonymical connection with the Vorrh. Throughout his journey, it turns Peter Williams into Oneofthewilliams. The Westerner becomes an Other via his journey in the Vorrh and being the wielder of the bow. From the point of view of space the native overcomes the colonizer, the female outdoes the male. From the standpoint of any-space-whatever, the Vorrh transforms him into Oneofthewilliams.

He becomes a legendary creature on whom the domination of the Vorrh has taken its toll: he has lost connection with his self and his sense of time and space. However, this dislocation does not annul his call to roam in the Vorrh and to search for a new owner of the weapon. When Ishmael and Williams meet in the forest, the former asks the latter how long has he been in the forest. Owing to the influence of the Vorrh as a space, Williams cannot grasp the meaning of time and space, which leads to Ishmael's conclusion that the Vorrh devoured the memory of Williams and his potential to meaning-making. The bow finds its new owner in Ishmael; Williams feels that the influence of the Vorrh changes in him, 'his memory of her [Irrinipeste] had shifted; they were no longer one body' (Catling, 2016, p. 409). Oneofthewilliams rambles around the Vorrh as an alien material in the space of the forest.

The Boundary Holder claims to be 'a servant to the Vorrh all of my life; I have tended to its needs and commands; I have engaged with its watchers and culled its predators' (490). He confronts Williams and decides to torture him in order to understand the monstrosity of the forest, the fantastical nature of the Vorrh and what holy monstrosity consists of. Williams is killed by 'the first arrow, the one that Este [Irrinipeste] had made for him' (Catling, 2016, p. 492) without telling his torturer anything. The reason why the Boundary Holder wants to have the knowledge of Oneofthewilliams points toward the presupposition that Peter Williams has heterotopian features that are related to the Vorrh or as Sarah K. Cantrell writes 'heterotopias remain separate from the places that surround them' (Cantrell, 2011, p. 205); thus, the altered Williams can no longer present information about the Vorrh because the system with which he could have constructed the forest as place has been shattered by every scrutinized point of view of the wilderness. The Vorrh as Fantastic of Place provides shelter to both pro-tagonists; its monstrosity derives from its shattered points of positionality (time and space). Even Oneofthewilliams has problems with identifying how many times he has crossed the forest; thus the visited fragments do not melt into one single spatial frame.

Although the Vorrh is the agent of transgression, later in the narrative this condition changes into the Fantastic of Place as well. As somebody who bears the features of the Deleuzian term, any-space-whatever, the cyclops metamorphoses himself in the forest into a normative person and a bow wielder. During his stay in the city, he was a lover and before a child. These aspects are all actualised potentials, no matter how contradictory they may seem. Consequently, on the level of point of view characters, this metonymi-cal connection between the bow made out of the woman and the Vorrh indicates the monstrosity of the forest by changing the wielder of the weapon into something he is originally not.

In Essenwald, Ishmael's peculiarity is being taken advantage of in a form of sex slavery by a woman named Ghertrude Eloise Tulp. He escapes from his confinement in order to discover the city of Essenwald. This getaway takes place during the time of a carnival, in which the residents of the city 'have a party to thank the forest for its gifts. It lasts for three days and nights, everybody stops work' (Catling, 2016, p. 171). This form of festivity bears features of the Foucauldian heterotopia, since these celebrations 'are not oriented toward the eternal, they are rather absolutely temporal' (Foucault, 1986, p. 26). As an Other, the cyclops protected by the masquerade copulates with a blind woman, who wears a mask. After the act she gets back her eyesight. When Ishmael wakes up next morning and tries to return home, he is attacked, but leaves his pursuers behind and flees into the Vorrh. In the forest, he is 'one of a multitude of strange things in this forest' (Catling, 2016, p. 369); consequently he is no longer an Other; and in there, he acquires the power of the colonizer, when he encounters then humbles the native hunter who is after Peter Williams:

> The cyclops lowered his face and looked into his subordinate's eyes; a great passion rose in him and swelled up, out of his chest. 'You are mine!' he boomed. His voice was commanding and alien to him, bred out of certainty and spite; the hunter shrivelled under its command, triggering some other instinct in Ishmael (Catling, 2016, p. 408).

As the new wielder of the weapon, the altered cyclops spots the way back and returns to Essenwald, a 'new application of meaning' emerges out of the Vorrh (Catling, 2016, p. 411). After Ishmael has been operated on to gain another eye, he reappears again in Essenwald, where he realises that 'Noth-ing had happened to his memory. He had suffered no adverse effect [in the forest]' (Catling, 2016, p. 466). His face becomes normative, full, a sign of the affection-image or as Deleuze states in *Cinema 1* 'the power-quality [which is] expressed by a face' (Deleuze, 1986, p. 110). Not only does the weapon convey the potentiality of the any-space-whatever, but Ishmael's face as well. As he chooses an another eye, he actualises the potential and loses its homogenity by becoming a power-wielding person. In Essenwald he is so absorbed 'in finding his place in his new life that he temporarily forgot his old one; he could hold no reflection on anything other than Cyrena [Lohr, the blind woman with whom he copulated earlier]. He longed for her to see his truth, not because he was deformed and rare, but, conversely, because of his growing normality and commonness' (Catling, 2016, p. 477).

Conclusion

Spatiality in Brian Catling's *The Vorrh* and its scrutiny proves to be difficult to tackle. The chapter scrutinized a mythical forest (Vorrh) and its relation to an European settlement (Essenwald) in the context of colonialism via the methods of spatiality from the point of view of point of world-building and from the aspect of two protagonists whose ontological and epistemological metamorphoses are assigned to the Vorrh itself. The wilderness is perceived as space according to the terminology of Patricia García and Yi-Fu Tuan, whereas the city is seen as place that is identified also via Garcían terms. The opposition the two locations constitute is also presented and explored by the dyad of holiness and monstrosity. Furthermore, another conflict is examined from the vantage point of colonialism in order to relate to the metaphorization of sexual territorialization in which the explorers are males who penetrate the Terra Incognita, the females. The Vorrh is seen as female, whereas the European colonizer as the male figure. In the connection between the Vorrh and Essenwald, balance of power favours the former. Essenwald is identified as a place with its organized life, ontologically and epistemologically comprehensible conduct of living. However, Vorrh is space 'conceived of as an abstract physical category composed of a set of relations and dimensions' (García, 2015, p. 21) and this chapter also relies on Yi-Fu Tuan's definition of space which is understood as open and by that it also means that it 'has no trodden paths and signposts. It has no fixed pattern of established human meaning' (Tuan, 1977, p. 54).

Apart from the above mentioned differentiations, the relation of the two locations can also be presented via the concepts of Foucault's heterotopia and Deleuze's any-space-whatever. These features pave the way for the metamorphoses of the two protagonists. The space of the Vorrh actualises the potentiality within the two main characters, Peter Williams and the cyclops, Ishmael. The colonist and the Other come from the place of Essenwald and enter the wilderness of Vorrh. The former turns into Oneofthewilliams, the chosen one, the messiah for the natives; the Vorrh turns the colonizer–native divide topsy-turvy, and constructs an Other from the Westerner. The latter becomes a non-Other, tamed, Western man with a pair of eyes. The explanation stems partly from the condition of the Vorrh as Fantastic of Space. That is a Garcían term, which is 'a literary phenomenon where the normal laws of physical space that rule our extratextual experience are not respected' (García, 2015, p. 26) and it functions as '*agent* of the transgression, provoking the breach of logical laws' (García, 2015, p. 33). The differentiation between Fantastic of Space and Fantastic of Place, 'space is seen as the *host* of the fantastic agent' (García, 2015, p. 33), has been overcome by the Vorrh, which bears both aspects of these Garcían notions. The former most resembles the Vorrh, whereas the latter is the city of Essenwald.

Although the forest that looms over the narrative not only obliterates two of the most important epistemological and ontological points (time and space), but also explodes into other signs that are metonymically connected to the Vorrh: the altered face of Ishmael and the bow made from Irrinipeste, the female seer of the natives. This chapter attempted to raise the issue of the characteristics of monstrosity and its relation to holiness. It aimed to examine their emergence from the two narrative spaces and settings through the ideas of Fantastic of Space and Fantastic of Place; of any-space-whatever and heterotopia. The extension of potential topics for examination in *The Vorrh* is constant. One cannot expect less from a forest that devours everything that it encounters in ways we would expect from a monster.

References

Cantrell, S. K., (2011). "'I solemnly swear I am up to no good': Foucault's Heterotopias and Deleuze's Any-Spaces-Whatever in J. K. Rowling's Harry Potter Series". *Children's Literature*, Volume 39, pp. 195–212.

Catling, B. (2016). *The Vorrh*. London: Hodder & Stoughton.

Deleuze, G. (1986). *Cinema 1: The Movement-Image*. Minneapolis: University of Minnesota Press.

Foucault, M. (1986). "Of Other Spaces". *Diacritics*, Vol. 16, No. 1 (Spring), pp. 22–27. Web. 5 June 2018.

García, P. (2015). *Space and the Postmodern Fantastic in Contemporary Literature The Architectural Void*. New York: Routledge.

Ryan, Marie-Laure. (1991). "Possible Worlds and Accessibility Relations: A Semantic Typology of Fiction." *Poetics Today* 12. 3 (Autumn): 553–576.

Tuan, Y. (1977). *Space and Place: The Perspective of Experience*. University of Minnesota Press.

Westphal, B. (2016). *The Plausible World: A Geocritical Approach to Space, Place, and Maps*. Springer.

Part 2

Denizens of the Woods

Chapter 4

Long in the Tooth?
Werewolves of a Certain Age

Jon Hackett

Judith Halberstam argues that 'Gothic novels [and horror films] are technologies that produce the monster as a remarkably mobile, permeable, and infinitely interpretable body' (Halberstam, 1995, p. 21). The intention of this paper is to take her assertion literally by examining special effects technologies and their contribution to a number of canonical werewolf films. Though some might dispute this assertion, I will argue that the heyday of screen werewolves was the 1980s; if this is true, then what are the implications of ageing for werewolf representation? Are the dazzling transformation scenes from 1980s werewolf cinema now dated and are these monsters superseded by 'younger' creatures facilitated by more recent special effects technologies?

There are four main sections in what follows. First, I will outline the wave of notable werewolf films in the early eighties and on, in order to highlight the prominence of this beast in the pop-cultural imaginary. Second, I will discuss the ways in which advances in special effects technologies facilitated on-screen representations of lycanthropes – and often featured prominently in discussions about and interest in werewolf films in this decade. I will then change tack and consider some ways of theorising machines that were developed in France in the mid to late part of the last century, making the case for these conceptions as possible frameworks in which to interpret the werewolf machines of 1980s cinema. I will finish by considering the question of the ageing of werewolves and their associated analogue technologies, with discussion of a recent film that thematises this in its narrative, namely *Late Phases* (Adrián García Bogliano, 2014).

Year of the Wolf

In fact, 1981 is the year that (nobody but) I am calling *annus lupi*, the year of the wolf. For it is in that year that the 1980s werewolf boom began, with three landmark films in the genre – *An American Werewolf in London* (John Landis, 1981), *The Howling* (Joe Dante, 1981) and *Wolfen* (Michael Wadleigh, 1981). The first two of these films, in particular, were also landmarks in their use of the analogue special effects technologies previously mentioned, including prosthetics and pneumatic devices – as well as involving artisanal workarounds that revealed the ingenuity of the special effects artists involved. Latex and synthetic compounds such as polyurethane were especially important in facilitating this work.

Rick Baker's work on *An American Werewolf in London* set the template for many of the transformation scenes in these films. Paul Davis's (2009) documentary, *Beware the Moon: Remembering An American Werewolf in London*, interviews Baker and his crew, as well as Landis and actor David Naughton, on how the iconic scene in Landis's film had been achieved. Landis required bright light for the shoot, which meant that the use of shadow to obscure awkward elements in the frame that horror film had relied on since the 1930s Universal cycle was not possible. Naughton was required to work on this scene for six days, ten hours a day; on one of the days he was stuck with his head joined to a prosthetic wolf body, the rest of his own body below an elevated stage built on the set.

On a couple of occasions, effects were used that highlighted the potential of these new analogue effects technologies. In particular, the extension or swelling of body parts that accompany the excruciating scene (in which Naughton's screaming never lets us forget the pain that this transformation involves for the character) stand out. An iconic production still that is often reproduced, sees Naughton holding his hand aloft, with the palm of the hand extending as his bones crack and stretch. This was effected through the insertion of a pneumatic ram improvised with syringes, into the moulded plastic hand model. In shot, due to the framing, the viewer cannot see that this hand is self-standing and not attached to the actor's own arm. Towards the end of the sequence, polyurethane head models of a progressively lupine Naughton were also stretched with syringes in an equally well-known profile shot of the muzzle extending into wolf form.

Davis's documentary makes clear how important improvisation and creativity were to effecting this scene. It was more viable to shoot the transformation more-or-less in reverse, since it was easier progressively to shave applied werewolf hair from Naughton's body than to add ever longer strands. In addition, an effect that sees hairs sprout rapidly from latex skin in close up, was achieved through pulling inserted hairs 'inside' the model and then reversing the footage to make them grow outwards.

Likewise, Jörg Bauer's (2004) making-of documentary, *Welcome to Werewolfland*, outlines the production history of *The Howling*. The latter film's director, Joe Dante, concedes that the transformation scene with no cutaway in this movie was 'the thing that got the picture made'. Rob Bottin was the special effects artist here who was responsible for the transformation of Robert Picardo into a wolfman, in front of the protagonist, played by Dee Wallace. This involved Picardo wearing a latex mask modelled on his own face, under which were inserted condoms that could be inflated to produce a bubbling effect; a bladder attached to his neck could also be inflated – with the unfortunate side effect of restricting the actor's breathing.

Experimentation was also a feature of this film, with footage speeded up and slowed down to accentuate particular moments of transformation. Happy accidents were achieved, such as sudden jolts in the transformations that although mistakes, could be turned into significant moments by adding bone-cracking sounds through foley to make sense of them as part of the morphing process.

Interestingly, both of these influential 1980s werewolf films shared special effects personnel. Rick Baker had jumped ship from Landis's film, when it appeared that *An American Werewolf in London* would not enter production any time soon. According to Dante, when Landis heard about *The Howling* he hastened to get his own picture under production, taking back Baker, not before the latter recommended Rob Bottin, his protégé, to Dante.

Analogous creatures emerged throughout the early to mid part of the decade, perhaps most notably the following year in John Landis's music video for Michael Jackson's 'Thriller', title song from an album which remains the world's best seller. Special effects were once again by Rick Baker. The video was itself a landmark in terms of its duration, production values and cultural prominence; it featured the singer transforming into a werewolf at the start of the video. Much to the hilarity of the then young author, UK television comedian Lenny Henry spoofed the 'Thriller' video in his BBC series (*The Lenny Henry Show*, BBC, 1984), reversing the transformation scene so that his sweetheart started screaming only once the wolf had transformed into Michael.

Other feature films that utilised werewolf special effects included *The Company of Wolves* (Neil Jordan, 1984), *The Beast Within* (Philippe Mora, 1981 – though I am perhaps taking liberties in considering the beast in this film to be a werewolf), *Silver Bullet* (Daniel Attias, 1985), *Teen Wolf* (Rod Daniel, 1985) and *The Monster Squad* (Fred Dekker, 1987). Aside from these examples there were also sequels for some of the films, including *Teen Wolf Too* (Christopher Leitch, 1987) and several for *The Howling*. The lycan-thrope, then, was a regular feature of 1980s horror films, video and television spoofs.

Some of these films had to skimp on the special effects sequences due to budget. *Silver Bullet*'s werewolf villain transforms in around 25 seconds flat, with cutaways and cutting back to a progressively more hirsute werewolf that recalls the earlier Universal cycle of films. When we have a recognisably werewolf face, it bulges at several points, presumably due to inflatable airbags beneath the prosthetic skin, amid much growling. At one point nails emerge from a hairy hand, rather like in the transformation sequences achieved by Stan Winston for the brief-lived television series *Manimal* (NBC, 1983). Amusingly, in this scene the beast dispatches his victim with a baseball bat instead of tooth and claw, rather as if to acknowledge the somewhat limited means with which they had to fabricate the werewolf itself.

Of course, this cycle of films in the 1980s was far from the first appearance of werewolves in film and in some ways we can see the films mentioned above in terms of a revival. Universal had released some key examples as part of their foundational cycle of horror films, such as *Werewolf of London* (Stuart Walker, 1935), *The Wolf Man* (Curt Wagner, 1941) and *Frankenstein Meets the Wolf Man* (Roy William Neill, 1943). When Universal – and Hollywood more broadly – tired of making horror films, perceiving audiences as lacking interest, independent American cinema produced examples such as *I Was a Teenage Werewolf* (Gene Fowler Jr., 1957).

Though the UK studio Hammer is often seen as capitalising on the market opportunity left by Hollywood's underestimation of interest in horror film in the late 1950s (see Hutchings, 2003), nonetheless among the films made by the studio in its heyday there is only one key lycanthropic example, *The Curse of the Werewolf* (Terence Fisher, 1961), though a notable one in the studio's output. Two of its rivals produced interesting examples from within British genre cinema: Tyburn with *Legend of the Werewolf* (Freddie Francis, 1975) and Amicus with *The Beast Must Die* (Paul Annett, 1974). The latter of these is particularly inventive, including elements from murder mysteries and, some have argued, Blaxploitation movies along with its werewolf antagonist. From other national popular cinemas we might point to the Spanish cycle of werewolf films featuring Paul Naschy.

Given this rich heritage, we might consider whether the 1980s werewolf movie was characteristic of the wider postmodern culture often associated with this decade. Indeed, this argument finds support in the association between these films and pop-cultural staples such as the teen movie, creature feature and rock'n'roll soundtrack. *An American Werewolf in London* was particularly effective in its ironic use of songs such as Bobby Vinton's 'Blue Moon', Credence Clearwater Revival's 'Bad Moon Rising' and Van Morrison's 'Moondance', and similar to *Jaws* (Steven Spielberg, 1975) – being a sort of big-budget exploitation movie (Wharton, 2013). *The Howling* can be seen like much of Joe Dante's cinema as an affectionate homage to 1950s creature features; we might compare it to other films by this director such as *Piranha* (1978), *Gremlins* (1984) or *Matinee* (1993) in this respect. In these films, parody and pastiche, intertextuality and irony, often feature – though thankfully not overriding the scares of the 1981 films, which often remain effective at this level too.

Prosthetics and SFX

An American Werewolf in London and *The Howling* ushered in a golden age of werewolf representations utilising makeup and prosthetics as well as pneumatic pumps. Other classic examples of the time include Landis's aforementioned video for 'Thriller' and *The Company of Wolves*. In these films, advances in effects pioneered by the likes of Rick Baker and Rob Bottin produce more mutable lycanthropes than the makeup technologies of earlier decades had allowed, for instance in the Universal or Hammer horror films. Above all, these effects facilitated bodily mutation, such as the iconic transformations in *An American Werewolf in London*, in which our hapless hero undergoes excruciating bodily warping into his werewolf alter ego. These sequences in the films were for many their most striking and certainly were at the centre of critical and audience interest in them.

In this respect, the striking special effects (SFX) sequences and audience fascination in them follow a time-honoured tradition for popular cinema, as highlighted by Bordwell, Thompson and Staiger in their classic work on Hollywood cinema:

> Indeed, special effects have exerted a perennial fascination for moviegoers, and popular magazines have never tired of showing how Hollywood wizardry could simulate bar-room brawls, snowstorms, sea battles, and earthquakes. The celebration of special effects is only a particular case of the tendency of Hollywood to promote technology as legerdemain. George Lucas's special effects firm is aptly named Industrial Light and Magic (Bordwell, Thompson & Staiger, 1988, p. 243).

As these authors specify, the example of George Lucas's work in *Star Wars* (1977) and other films were the most prominent examples of popular cinema's increasing privileging of effects as spectacle at the time. The industry, as they highlight, is keen to foster this type of screen pleasure in audiences, as evidenced in copious making-of documentaries released with blockbuster DVD releases.

However, the sort of special effects under discussion in this chapter provided a sort of alternative artisanal aesthetic that also proved effective with audiences. There were precursors for this type of practice in the much-admired stop-motion work of Willis O'Brien in *King Kong* (Merian C. Cooper & Ernest B. Schoedsack, 1933) or Ray Harryhausen's various films. Like these revered pioneers, for werewolf special effects artists such as Baker and Bottin, there was scope to shine as individual artists. As Turnock observes, 'In spite of the 1970s effort towards a seamless photorealistic aesthetic, the small flurry of feature films making use of traditional stop motion suggests that there was something of a practitioner backlash against ILM's homogenization stance.' (Turnock, 2015, p. 243)

Consequently, for a short time at least, certain effects practitioners attained near auteur status; for some spectators their work was at least as interesting as that of the director. That is, Rick Baker, Rob Bottin and Tom Savini (the latter more involved with stalkers and zombies than werewolves), Dick Smith (for *The Exorcist*, William Friedkin, 1973) and Stan Winston (especially in science fiction) had attained status analogous perhaps to Busby Berkeley in the 1930s Warner musicals – rivalling the esteem accorded the notional directors in which their sequences featured. Lisa Purse summarises the appeal of this aesthetic compared with the industrial mode of production of ILM:

> The move away from a seamless optical composite took a particular form in the vein of unapologetically low-budget horror and sci-fi movies popular in the period, which showcased a vivid mixture of prosthetics, makeup effects, puppetry, animatronics, and stop-motion work (Purse, 2016: 147).

The ascendancy of the artisan SFX artist was consecrated with the Oscar award to Rick Baker for *An American Werewolf in London*. Famously, a new award category was created in order to recognise his contribution to the film. The reputation of films like this and *The Howling* retains a fascination with the accomplished special effects, as evidenced by special edition DVDs and making-of videos; as well as discussion on commentary tracks. Even if the cutting-edge feel of the effects technologies have passed in the wake of CGI, there remains a type of fascination with the accomplishments of previous analogue technologies for many spectators that one might compare with the work of Harryhausen – although the latter's stop-motion skeletons, dinosaurs and classical beasts may not appear photorealistically convincing in our era, the inventiveness and craft retain a charm for many as well as being acknowledged by the likes of James Cameron and Steven Spielberg as a crucial influence on their later digital effects (see for example their comments in Gilles Penso's (2011) documentary, *Ray Harryhausen: Special Effects Titan*).

The rise of CGI in the end has largely eclipsed the role of these artisanal SFX artists who were such a feature of popular genre cinema in the 1980s. As Turnock (2015) observes, George Lucas's ILM and Peter Jackson's Weta Workshop have had the effect of effacing the contributions of the individual practitioners, now subsumed into a larger industrial mode of production. It is frequently the directors such as Cameron and Jackson who are identified as the key auteurs behind the visual effects in their blockbusters. Nonetheless, as we shall see later, there remain films, usually independent cinema for specific genre audiences, that continue to utilise practical analogue effects in their films. Spectators of these films often relish the in-camera techniques with a sort of cinephilic (or paracinematic perhaps) appreciation of the artisanal techniques largely absent from digital blockbuster cinema. We shall see a productive example of this that taps into the cinephile pleasures of the 1980s werewolf cycle in the discussion of Bogliano's *Late Phases* in the final section of this chapter.

Theorising the Machine

As we have seen, in the era in question, advances in technologies associated with special effects facilitated the revival of werewolf representations on screen, while allowing for transformation scenes that had been impossible in earlier eras. In this section, I will take a step back and consider ways of conceiving of this fruitful coincidence of technological advance with a cultural interest once more in lycanthropes. Though the following discussion may seem abstract, it will at least model one way (or a set of comparable ways) for accounting for the coincidence of technological with cultural or aesthetic determinants.

Here we will go back to some ideas that were being advanced in French philosophical debates on technology, technics and vitalism in the middle of the twentieth century. What these discussions have in common is, at various levels, a wish to avoid strict binaries between mechanism and vitalism, and elements and their structures, in favour of a more all-encompassing model to account for the genesis of technologies and machines. It is hoped that the relevance of these frameworks for the current discussion will become more apparent later in this section.

Perhaps a quotation from one of these thinkers, Georges Canguilhem, will begin to make the relevance of these debates a little clearer:

> Indeed, the problem of the relations between machine and organism has generally been studied only in one direction: almost always, the attempt has been to explain the structure and function of the organism on the basis of the structure and function of an already-constructed machine. Only rarely has anyone sought to understand the very construction of the machine on the basis of the structure and function of the organism (Canguilhem, 2008, pp. 75–76).

Canguilhem's work often considers vitalism as a philosophy of science, and questions the frequent privileging of mechanism as an explanatory mechanism over this alternative tradition. Here, it might make us consider for a moment whether the only option in accounting for our prosthetic and animatronic beasts is in terms of the development of machines and their associated mechanisms. Might we conversely account for the genesis of the machines on the basis of a wider cultural lycanthropy?

To continue these ideas a little further, we can turn to Gilbert Simondon's philosophy of technics. In *Du mode d'existence des objets techniques*, Simondon writes: 'The beginning of a lineage of technical objects is marked by a synthetic act of invention that is basic to a technical essence' (Simondon, 2007, p. 22). We can perhaps see the prosthetics and pneumatic devices of *An American Werewolf in London* as inaugurating a lineage of technical werewolf objects that in its decade was productive of new exciting lycanthropes on screen. Simondon considers that the 'lineage of technical objects' has a sort of determinant role in producing further examples. This is because in a certain sense, the becoming and individuation of machines and technical objects is always linked to an 'associated milieu' from which further examples may arise.

This associated milieu is conceived in the widest sense; here it might encompass advances in make-up, prosthetics and animatronics; a cinephile or paracinematic interest in special effects, both big budget and industrial, and low-budget and artisanal; an ongoing audience for horror, cult and genre cinema; and perhaps a series of ideas around masculinity in crisis that have often been associated with readings of werewolf narratives in recent decades.

We can see related concerns in the work of Félix Guattari, the psychoanalyst and (anti-) psychiatrist mostly associated with his work with Gilles Deleuze. It is in particular two of Guattari's individual works that I want to elucidate some analogous ideas. First, from 1969 there is his article, 'Machine and Structure', which appears in the collection, *Psychoanalysis and Transversality* (2015). Here, Guattari conceives of a machine as an irreducible element that escapes structure, which can be related to a general structure (such as language or signification) only at the level of a rupture or event. Such an element occurs as a singularity; as an event in history (inaugurating the era associated with a particular machines); or at the level of individual subjectivity: 'The human being is caught where the machine and the structure meet' (Guattari, 1995, p. 322). This latter emphasis is present in the desiring-machines of his later works with Deleuze. Guattari wishes to keep the definition of machine general, to allow it play this topological role at various levels, subjective, cultural, political or social.

The machine plays an important part, too, in Guattari's later work, *Chaosmosis*, published after his two books with Deleuze, *Anti-Oedipus* and *A Thousand Plateaus*. In fact, it reworks some ideas from these collaborations while retaining some of the previous emphasis in 'Machine and Structure'. Here, we can see an echo of Simondon's ideas of a lineage of technical objects with its associated milieu, in Guattari's conception of an abstract machine.

> For our part, we would like to resituate semiology within the scope of an expanded, machinic conception which would free us from a simple linguistic opposition between Expression/Content, and allow us to integrate into enunciative assemblages an indefinite number of substances of Expression, such as biological codings or organisational forms belonging to the socius (Guattari, 1995, pp. 23–24).

In order to elaborate this concept we could appeal to various types of coding such as DNA perhaps; or structures of chemical elements. These appear to combine a structure of symbols or signifying elements; with a concrete presence in matter itself. Here, notions of on the one hand, a code, structure or series of signs; and on the other, real-world, concrete referents (or signifieds); are present on the same plane. As Anne Sauvagnargues argues: 'The machine is no longer a technical object, but is rather the operative philosophical concept that explains how three components – matter, thought and brain – may function together while remaining heterogeneous' (Sauvagnargues, 2016, p. 190).

At this level, the abstract machine is further specified by Guattari as 'diagrammatic' (Guattari, 1995, p. 34). In this respect, Sauvagnargues highlights that terms such as machine, diagram, machinic assemblage, apparatus and so on, play comparable roles (with certain differences) in the work of Foucault as well as Deleuze and Guattari (and we might add Lyotard). There is a common emphasis in finding concepts that can simultaneously be defined abstractly while playing a concrete role in the genesis of wider technological, social, cultural and political formations.

Wolves in the Machine

So far so abstract – but what does all this discussion of machines suggest in relation to the 1980s special effects technologies? For some readers the relevance will not be clear. Nonetheless, it can be argued that this non-structuralist and non-mechanistic analysis of machines that was taking place in the mid to late 20th century allows us to articulate the wide set of determinants we might identify with regard to werewolf representations on screen.

This type of explanation, then, will posit a sort of abstract lycanthropic machine at work in the 1980s and onwards, that inaugurated (through the event of *annus lupi*) a technical lineage of werewolf machines in cinema. Furthermore, this technical lineage of objects would be inextricable from an associated milieu, which would take in various social and cultural realms, including advances in plastics, animatronics and synthetic compounds; a postmodern fondness for returning to classic horror and paracinema such as creature features; a possible fascination with masculinity in crisis, for which the wolf would provide a ready metaphor (this is carried yet further in *Wolf* (Mike Nichols, 1994) in the decade that follows. All of these phenomena taken together might be considered as a sort of generalised cultural lycanthropy that mutually conditioned both the particular special effects and machines in the films I have been discussing as well as the appeal that werewolves evidently provided for audiences in the decade under question.

We can extend this cultural lycanthropy to the spectatorial pleasures involved in watching these films as well as in the time-honoured fascination viewers have in finding out about how the particular effects have been achieved. Simondon argues that our intuition of technical objects is part of the same process that produces the objects themselves. This is the process that Simondon refers to as transduction. 'Transduction is not only an ontological category, then. It also designates the method of thought itself. As a method, the transduction does not remain outside thought' (De Bestegui, 2013, p. 173). Technical objects, if the reader will, are produced at the same time as understanding in the viewer, through this process of transduction that overcomes the barrier between thought and being.

The perhaps strange consequence of this is that the invention of on-screen werewolves is, conceived on this level, part of the same process as our intuition of them (as enlightened spectators). If this is the case, then we can argue that werewolf cinephilia is part of the same process as on-screen lycanthropy itself. The transformations that torment the protagonists of these films are shared, albeit at a virtual level rather than quite so painfully and concretely, by the viewer, as part of the 'invention' of this lineage of technical werewolf objects.

Late Phases

Some of the machines considered in this chapter, whether prosthetic, animatronic or abstract, may seem to have had their day. For some, the more conceptual sections of this discussion might appear a little old hat too. More seriously still, the in-camera special effects associated with the 1980s werewolf cycle have largely been superseded by transformation sequences that are achieved in post-production through digital technologies. The question must be asked – does the age of CGI monsters make werewolves appear obsolete?

Digital werewolves have indeed appeared on screen in series such as the *Twilight* and *Underworld* films. One might also cite Joe Johnston's (2010) *The Wolfman*. To assert their inferiority or otherwise to the 1980s practical effects-based creatures would be a matter of taste, presumably aligned to various cinephile or paracinematic pleasures, probably related also to one's generation and possible nostalgic impulses. There are also aspects of horror film fandom that occasionally encourage investments in particular time-honoured techniques; here I merely adduce anecdotal evidence of the rounds of applause that often greet directors in Q&A sessions in horror film festivals, when they profess a loyalty to practical rather than digital effects technologies. Perhaps one reason for the popularity of *Dog Soldiers* (Neil Marshall, 2002) among some fans of the genre was the prevalent use of make-up, prosthetics and animatronics alongside the presence of digital.

One recent werewolf film that favours practical over computerised effects allows the practical effects werewolf to age gracefully from this perspective. *Late Phases* (Adrian Garcia Bogliano, 2014) relocates the werewolf film to a retirement home. Nick Damici plays a blind Vietnam veteran, Ambrose McKinley, who is moved to the home by his son. Soon after moving in, on the night of the full moon, McKinley's house is broken into and his dog killed. After this, a succession of residents from the home start to disappear; McKinley tries to track down the killer. He clearly suspects a werewolf is responsible since goes to the local gun shop in the hope of getting some silver bullets made.

In this respect, *Late Phases* bears an interesting similarity with *The Beast Must Die* (Paul Annett, 1972) produced by the British studio Amicus. Despite the very different feel and milieux of these films, they both combine elements of the whodunnit with the werewolf film. Both films involve a central sleuth character tracking down a lycanthrope from among a limited number of suspects in a relatively isolated location surrounded by forest.

Both protagonists are differentiated from their suspects on the basis of their identity and temperament. Tom Newcliffe in the earlier film, played by Calvin Lockhart, is a self-made millionaire and big-game hunter, who has escaped the 'stinking shanty towns' of his birth (the location is unspecified), to find himself among middle and upper-class Brits. He is also marked out by them by his near maniacal obsession with hunting down the titular beast, however dangerous this may be for himself and the rest of his guests. In the case of *Late Phases*, Ambrose McKinley is a curmudgeonly figure who clearly enjoys a difficult relationship with his son who has despatched him to the retirement home. The chain-smoking vet also appears differentiated from many of the community in his clear indifference to the middle-class propriety of his neighbours.

My main interest here in this film is in its use of low-budget special effects technologies to produce both on-screen werewolves and the transformation sequences beloved in these films. In one key scene, we witness the revelation of the killer in a scene that involves his on-screen morphing in his own front room in the retirement home, before another of the possible suspects. This of course brings to mind the earlier change scenes in *An American Werewolf in London* and *The Howling*. This is all the more so since the scene obviously uses practical effects based on make-up and prosthetics, rather than achieving the scene through digital visual effects alone.

Once more, there is a helpful making-of documentary, *Early Phases*, on the DVD release, which outlines the contribution of the Kurtzman special effects studio to the film. One part of the transformation of Lance Guest into werewolf sees the actor tear off a silicone mask of himself in order to reveal the werewolf 'underneath', which is a pleasingly ironic reversal of the 'man in wolf suit' stereotype of the pre-1980s cinematic wolfman. This is achieved through motion control photography, stitching together 10 shots with some use of digital; on the DVD commentary, Bogliano explains that he used this as a way of shooting such a scene differently to a standard cut to reaction shot and back. This makes the transformation sequence appear to be shot on a single take, with the camera panning and tilting between the two characters instead of cutting. However, it is in-camera techniques of make-up, prosthetics and animatronics that render the werewolf and the transformation, rather than digital visual effects, providing a continuity with the 1980s landmarks.

Here we may productively allude again to Julie A. Turnock's discussion of the aesthetics of Ray Harryhausen. Although the films I am discussing use different techniques, namely make-up, prosthetics and animatronics, instead of stop-motion, there is a comparison to be drawn between the spectatorial pleasures on offer in each case. This hinges on the viewer's acknowledgement that the insertion of the effect in the footage is 'visible' (and not seamless, as is the objective in photorealistic SFX); but that this need not, according to one's sensibility, detract from the enjoyment of the scene or sequence:

> Taking a cue from Harryhausen, I am calling the cinematic fantasy aesthetic that combines conventional live-action movie-making with 'unrealistic' animated material *'not-too-realism.'* 'Not-too-realism' interrogates how stop-motion balances the animated object with live-action footage. It engrosses the viewer into the diegesis not through its seamlessness, but by riveting the viewer through an amazement and appreciation of the artistry and effort of its handcraftedness (Turnock, 2015, pp. 242–243).

I would maintain that the use of practical effects in werewolf films might be enjoyed in the same way. That is, for some spectators at least, there is an available pleasure in observing how the transformation into the werewolf has been achieved through practical craft, with perhaps an intertextual pleasure in comparing these means with the previous work of Baker, Bottin, Winston and others. Bonus features and other paratexts evidence an interest in these techniques as creative responses to diegetic challenges, often achieved with limited means in independent genre cinema. One must qualify this assertion that such spectatorial pleasure will likely be circumscribed by the taste of the viewer. Those who have grown up in the CGI era may find it difficult to enjoy special effects sequences that look less 'real' to them if this is judged in terms of verisimilitude based on photorealistic standards.

Conclusion

I hope to have argued for the significance of this cycle of 1980s werewolf films, as well as their ongoing fascination for some viewers, even if this might be related to certain types of nostalgia or a certain type of sympathy with possibly outmoded techniques. Though digital effects claim the interest of many in the blockbuster cinema of Hollywood, nonetheless in certain independent cinema examples, the techniques pioneered by the likes of Baker, Bottin and Winston live on; indeed, advances in animatronics and silicone make related techniques in a sense easier than ever. I have advanced certain theoretical ideas about machines, technical objects and their evolution that may have tested the patience of certain readers; nonetheless, the aim was to see past the bits and bobs that make up on-screen werewolves and instead see these latter beasts as part of a wider techno-socio-cultural phenomenon.

Finally, we turned to Bogliano's recent film that acts at least in part as a homage to the 1980s cycle of werewolf films. My contention is that films such as this evidence the ongoing pleasures that are available in transformation scenes involving practical special effects based on make-up, prosthetics and animatronics. At the same time, it shows witty self-reflexivity in situating the diegesis in a retirement home, as if to acknowledge the possibly old-fashioned nature of the techniques used in its production. With its nostalgia-tinged appeal to the age of 1980s prosthetics, *Late Phases* thematises the ageing of analogue werewolves in its narrative. It is possible in this film for the pre-CGI werewolf to bow out with dignity.

Bibliography

Bordwell, D., Staiger, J. & Thompson, K. (1988), *The Classical Hollywood Cinema: Film Style and Mode of Production to 1960*, London & New York: Routledge.

Canguilhem, G. (2008 [1965]), *Knowledge of Life*, New York: Fordham University Press.

De Bestegui, M. (2012), 'Science and Ontology: From Merleau-Ponty's "Reduction" to Simondon's "Transduction"' in De Boever, A., Murray, A., Roffe, J. & Woodward, A. (eds), *Gilbert Simondon: Being and Technology*, Edinburgh: Edinburgh University Press.

Guattari, F. (2015 [1969]), 'Machine and Structure' in *Psychoanalysis and Transversality: Texts and Interviews 1955–1971*, Los Angeles: Semiotext(e).

Guattari, F. (1995 [1992]), *Chaosmosis: An Ethico-Aesthetic Paradigm*, Bloomington & Indianapolis: Indiana University Press.

Halberstam, J. (1995), *Skin Shows: Gothic Horror and the Technology of Monsters*, Durham: Duke University Press.

Hutchings, P. (2003), *Dracula*, London: I.B. Tauris.

Purse, L. (2016), 'The New Hollywood, 1981–1999: Special/Visual Effects' in Keil, C. & Whissel, K. (eds), *Editing and Special/Visual Effects*, New Brunswick: Rutgers University Press.

Sauvagnargues, A. (2016), *Artmachines: Deleuze, Guattari, Simondon*, Edinburgh: Edinburgh University Press.

Simondon, G. (2001 [1958]), *Du mode d'existence des objets techniques*, Paris: Aubier.

Turnock, J. (2015), *Plastic Reality: Special Effects, Technology, and the Emergence of 1970s Blockbuster Aesthetics*, New York: Columbia University Press.

Wharton, S. 2013, 'Welcome to the (Neo) Grindhouse! Sex, violence and the indie film' in King, G., Molloy, C. & Tzioumakis, Y. (eds) *American Independent Cinema: Indie, Indiewood and Beyond*, London & New York: Routledge.

Chapter 5

Cruising the Queer Forest with Alain Guiraudie: Woods, Plastics, Plasticities

Benjamin Dalton

If you go down to the woods today, you're sure of a queer surprise. The films of the contemporary French filmmaker and novelist Alain Guiraudie explore queer life and community across the rural landscapes of the South of France, foregrounding the forest as a nexus of queer gathering, dwelling and transformation. Guiraudie's forests have a queer gravitational pull: groups of men are drawn to the forest to have sex, escape, form communities, grow aphrodisiac crops or simply get lost. Besides offering pleasure and nourishment, these forests have a darker side, in which to take a walk in the woods is also to risk disorientation, loss and even murder. Both nurturing and destructive, Guiraudie's forests are dark utopias in which new, ambivalent forms of queer life and ecology are left to grow wild.

Guiraudie's first full-length feature, *No Rest for the Brave* (2003), depicts the oneiric wanderings of the protagonist Basile who is convinced he will die if he falls asleep; never fully knowing what is real and what is fantasy, Basile moves between villages to plateaus and forests, the trees enclosing spaces of communion between multiple identities and dimensions. Meanwhile, *The King of Escape* (2009) follows Armand, a gay tractor salesman, who escapes police by running into the forest, discovering there that other men from his town are cultivating a new kind of plant, which when consumed, metamorphoses and turbocharges libido and pleasure. The internationally acclaimed *Stranger by the Lake* (2013) takes place at a cruising beach next to a forest where men meet for erotic encounters under the cover of the trees; with the arrival of the mysterious Michel, this erogenous undergrowth later becomes the site of a string of brutal murders. *Staying Vertical* (2016) follows the travels of Léo, a screenwriter with writer's block; caring for his newborn child alone and sexually entangled with various men in the village, Léo takes refuge in the forest as a place of escape, healing and inspiration. Guiraudie's queer forests, then, comprise hybrid spaces for their human inhabitants, providing both protection and exposure, cultivation and annihilation.

Beyond the particular locale of the forest, commentators have noted the importance of landscape and nature in Guiraudie's films. Nathan Friedman, Eugenie Brinkema and Enda McCaffrey, for instance, explore variably how

Guiraudie's landscapes and outside spaces map pleasure, violence and queerness as elements of topology, topography and geography (Friedman, 2016; Brinkema, 2018; McCaffrey, 2019); Dion Kagan describes the 'partly anthropological and partly folkloric' space of the cruising site in *Stranger* as 'an idyllic landscape that is both out of synch with, and out of sight from, the rest of the world' (Kagan, 2013, p. 37); and Saige Walton, also with reference to *Stranger*, argues that 'plotlines, characters and different affective energies are all choreographed according to the lake's environment', theorising a 'highly rhythmic ecology' of spacings and syncopations between human bodies, their natural surroundings, and nonhuman forms of organic life (Walton, 2018, pp. 241, 246).

This chapter, however, locates Guiraudie's forests at the epicentre of his filmic landscapes as a privileged site of queer dwelling and cultivation. Indeed, the forest is an inescapable presence in Guiraudie's films. Even when the action is not set directly in the forest, the forest is always waiting on the periphery of the frame, simultaneously welcoming and menacing. From the trees always looming outside windows in *No Rest for the Brave*, to the forested horizons in *The King of Escape* and *Staying Vertical* that border all villages and fields, to the cruising forest in *Stranger* that provides cover for sexual encounters, the forest is unavoidable, omnipresent and magnetic. Beyond the human narratives sheltered under their canopies, Guiraudie's forests are vital characters in their own rights, existing in excess of and even in defiance of their queer human inhabitants; the camera often focuses on vegetation over human life and characters' dialogues regularly revolve around off-screen animal or environmental events. If Marie-Claire Loiselle argues that Guiraudie's films leave the viewer with the uncanny feeling that something larger is going on beyond the frame (Loiselle, 2002, p. 16), nowhere is this more true than in the forest, where a queer biodiversity of animal, insect, vegetal and geological beings constantly threaten to swallow human narratives and continue in their absence.

Cruising the queer woods, I explore how Guiraudie's forests constitute spaces in which questions of queer identity and experience emerge as inextricably connected with the mutability and plasticity of nonhuman life forms and environmental processes. I argue that Guiraudie's mapping of queer bodies through forestscapes provocatively cross-fertilises *queer* with *nature* in a way that reinvents the queer–nature relationship and responds to certain critical impasses across the fields of queer theory, queer film and queer ecology. This cross-fertilisation resists any essentialisation or naturalisation of queer identities and bodies, and instead opens both 'queerness' and 'nature' up to unpredictable forms and mutations.

Guiraudie, Queer Ecology and Queer Plasticity

Nick Rees-Roberts sees Guiraudie as an antidote to a perceived stalemate in mainstream queer cinema in which '[t]he gay romantic narrative has seemingly reached a dead-end' in its 'transition from invisible to visible to commercially hypervisible and socially assimilated' (Rees-Roberts, 2015, p. 439). Whereas queer cinema's subversive and political bite once lay in its capacity to make visible marginal and exiled bodies and communities, the mainstream assimilation of queer cultures seems to have robbed filmic queer narratives of their transgressive or political agency. Searching for a 'capacious understanding of "queer"' which 'is preoccupied with more than same-sex identities and spaces' (440), Rees-Roberts suggests that Guiraudie's films counteract queer cinema's commercialised impotency precisely through their attention to 'the types of places, milieus, and bodies, which tend to be overlooked by more mainstream production' as well as an 'experimental preoccupation with the aesthetic shapes, generic codes, and conceptual patterns of queer sexuality, bypassing social-realist cinema's more conventional mirror-image of contemporary France' (458).

Similarly, Damon R. Young argues that Guiraudie's films resist the appropriation of the queer subject under neoliberalism through a return to cinema in an age of digital surveillance: 'The battles of gay liberation already having been won, Guiraudie is free to be Hitchcock' (Young, 2018, p. 231). Young's attention to how *Stranger*'s 'bucolic setting' participates in the film's resistance to digital surveillance (216); and Rees-Roberts's foregrounding of Guiraudie's non-metropolitan spaces often forgotten by queer cinema (Rees-Roberts, 2015); I argue, invite further attention to Guiraudie's 'natural' spaces. Where Rees-Roberts, drawing from Bersani and Dutoit's *Forms of Being* (2004), briefly alludes to the 'visual correspondence between human and non-human life' (457) in *Stranger*, I argue that this 'non-human life' demands further exploration as a potentiality for queer ecosystems and ecologies.

Like Rees-Roberts and Young, Enda McCaffrey examines ways in which Guiraudie's novel *Now The Night Begins* (2018) counters a tendency for abstraction in queer theory, which forgets the lived experience of queer lives and bodies, de-sexualises queer politics, and founds its politics in negativity and anti-futurity (McCaffrey, 2016, p. 60). The queer negativity that McCaffrey is alluding to is the 'antisocial thesis' developed in works such as Lee Edelman's *No Future* (2004), in which Edelman argues against 'reproductive futurism' (Edelman, 2004, p. 26), promoting an explosion of all 'positive' forms, identifications and structures, in particular heterosexist notions of what constitutes 'natural' family and social bonds (41).

Wendy Moffat, like McCaffrey, argues against the abstraction of negativity, suggesting that queer theory has occluded its own capacity for change and transformation in forgetting the lived experiences and narratives of individual queer autobiographies, bypassing the unpredictable forms and transformations undergone in individual queer lived experience (Moffat, 2015). For McCaffrey, Guiraudie's queerness is 'not locked into a structure or identity but drifts as a sexuality [...] with the capacity to radicalise the Symbolic and also transform itself' (McCaffrey, 2016, pp. 68–69). McCaffrey's reading of Guiraudie replaces queer negativity with logics of preservation, transformation and futurity.

These logics, I suggest, counter Edelman's anti-future/anti-nature negativity precisely in recalling environmental and ecological calls for conservation and cultivation. Whilst McCaffrey's reading of *Now The Night Begins* does not examine Guiraudie's interest in natural landscape or ecology, his analysis of *Staying Vertical* elsewhere is interested in the film's attention to 'air, wind, water, land, sea, grass and trees' by which '[n]ature participates in and gives way to a transcendence of relations' (McCaffrey, 2019). I am interested in pushing these relations and their potential for transformation and mutation further in relation to theories of queer ecology and biology.

Beyond Guiraudie, the growing field of 'queer ecology' re-interrogates the perceived incompatibility between queerness and nature encouraged by 'antisocial' theorists like Edelman. Catriona Mortimer-Sandilands and Bruce Erickson demonstrate how this disconnect derives from the age-old designation of queerness as 'against nature' (Mortimer-Sandilands & Erickson, 2010, pp. 1–39). 'Nature' has long been ideologically aligned with normative conceptions of sex, gender and reproduction; politically suspect environmentalisms continue to uphold an 'eco(hetero)normativity' that views non-reproductive queer bodies as environmental threats (Di Chiro, 2010, pp. 202), '[taking] up the task of the racialized, gendered, and sexual marking of certain bodies as toxic' (Gosine, 2010, pp. 151).

Queer ecology thus underscores the importance of queering environmental, biological, and ecological discourses whilst emphasising how these same discourses might help us discover the queerness inherent in nature itself. Myra J. Hird, for instance, looks to the sexual diversity of fungi and microbacteria as evidence of 'the abundant queer behavior of most of the living matter on this planet' (Hird, 2004, p. 88). Timothy Morton hopes to find for queer theory 'a strange friend in nonessentialist biology', proclaiming that 'ecology is queer theory and queer theory is ecology' (Morton, 2010a, pp. 275, 281). Mortimer-Sandilands and Erickson suggest that we must invent 'an ecology that embraces deviation and strangeness as a necessary part of biophilia, sexual pleasure and transgression as foundational to environmental ethics and politics, and resistance to heteronormativity as part and parcel of ecological science and green strategy alike' (Mortimer-Sandilands & Erickson, 2010, p. 39). Countering Edelman's anti-futurity directly on environmental terms, Nicole Seymour hopes for a queer ecology 'in which futurity and future-thinking can function as queer ecological values' that show capitalism itself to be the real enemy of futurity, whilst demonstrating that queer theory's 'shirking of stable identities, epistemologies, and ontologies [...] might lend itself most effectively to empathetic, politicized advocacy for the non-human natural world' (Seymour, 2013, pp. 183, 184).

Whilst queer ecology looks to natural diversity to topple normative or essentialising structures and identities, there is a relative lack of discussion of the transformability or mutability of individual organisms themselves. This seems odd at a time when research into 'plasticity' and 'neuroplasticity' is exploding across the life sciences, particularly biology and neurosciences, which the philosopher Catherine Malabou argues have established plasticity as the 'style of an era' or the '*hermeneutic motor scheme* of an epoch' (Malabou, 2010, pp. 1, 13, original emphasis). From her celebration of the brain's neuroplasticity as a resource for freedom in *What Should We Do With Our Brain?* (2008) to her analysis of the plastic mutability of bodies, sexualities, and even machines across diverse and interdisciplinary works from *Changing Difference* (2011) to *Morphing Intelligence* (2019), Malabou seeks to demonstrate that all organic life is 'plastic' and able to transform itself ceaselessly.

With reference to the field of epigenetics, which explores how organisms mutate at the level of gene expression, Malabou states that 'biology is not essentialist' (Malabou, 2011, p. 139). She continues: 'there are no grounds for a concept of essence, conceived of as substance, be it ontological or natural. Transformability is at work from the start, it trumps all determination. Everything starts with metamorphosis' (ibid.). Queer ecology's overlooking of plasticity in its celebration of natural diversity, I suggest, risks paradoxically casting this natural diversity as itself unchanging and immutable. In insisting on the plasticity of plurality and diversity itself, Malabou can help us think a natural diversity that is itself constantly diversifying and metamorphosing.

Unlike what Greg Garrard terms 'the debilitating biophobia of queer theory' (Garrard, 2010, p. 79), Malabou, like many queer ecologists, freely embraces the biological as a privileged site for de-essentialisation or denaturalisation of nature itself. Whilst Malabou's principle focus in *Changing Difference* is the potential of plastic biology to rethink feminist politics and embodiment, the work of Michael Washington has brilliantly suggested the impact that Malabou's plasticisation of essence might offer queer theory and politics more broadly (Washington, 2017; 2018). Further, Jayna Brown draws from Malabou's plasticity in conceptualising 'the queerness of the biological' as that which resists hegemonic scientific discourses; beyond Malabou, a true 'plasticity of life' promises 'new forms of sociality and modes of being' (Brown, 2015, pp. 323, 337).

Like Washington and Brown, I also want to extend the queer resonances of Malabou's plasticity, this time through dialogues with queer ecology and cinema. Whilst the latency of (neuro)plasticity and epigenetics, or even Malabou herself, within queer ecologies points to fertile avenues for future exploration, so too does the latency of ecological or environmental attention to Malabou's own thought. Guiraudie's forests, I wager, provide fertile soils for this cross-cultivation.

This chapter cruises the transgressive biologies and plastic natures of Guiraudie's queer forest with Malabou and queer ecology as guides. First, I examine how Guiraudie himself imagines atmospheres of alienation and staleness within queer communities and lives mimicking those described above in queer theory, cinema and ecology, focusing on the disaffected or deserted cruising sites of *The King of Escape* and *Stranger*. Then I consider how spaces find themselves within or on the borders of woods and forests that harbor the potentiality to fertilise and cultivate new modes of queer existence and queer storytelling in *Staying Vertical*. If George Monbiot promotes a 'rewilding of natural ecosystems' as 'not an attempt to restore them to any prior state, but to permit ecological processes to resume' (Monbiot, 2013, p. 8); and Jack Halberstam and Tavia Nyong'o invite future reconceptualisations of 'wildness' that 'bewilder' sovereign structures, pronouncing it 'time to rewild theory' (Halberstam & Nyong'o, 2018, p. 454); I argue Guiraudie's forests initiate processes of queer rewilding that open queer ecologies up to unknown futures.

Faded Queer Utopias and the Promise of the Woods

The cruising sites and practices of *The King of Escape* and *Stranger by the Lake* are structured around forests. In *The King of Escape*, the cruising site is marked by a small carpark on the edge of forest where men meet before entering the woods together. Meanwhile, in *Stranger*, cruising occurs across the connected spaces of the carpark, forest, beach and lake, whereby men meet on the beach before again heading into the trees to fuck. An atmosphere of erotic ambivalence pervades these cruising sites where men circulate and have sex with a mixture of disinterest and ecstasy. The cruising site is thus presented as a space of alienation and affective decay on the one hand and the promise of transformative pleasure on the other. This ambivalence is echoed in readings of the cruising site in *Stranger* as variably Edenic (Kermabon, 2013, p. 10), a cursed utopia (Roy, 2013, p. 61) and as a 'queer u/dys-topia' (Young, 2018, p. 216).

If cruising had once been the anarchic and transgressive practice of transgression and *jouissance* celebrated by queer theorists as a mode of queer community-forming (see, for example, José Esteban Muñoz's hunting for 'ghosts of public sex' as 'queer utopian remembrance' (2009, pp. 33, 35), these practices and spaces are now pictured to have lost their political and orgasmic bite. This sexual alienation or disaffection, I argue, is seen to be inextricable from a disconnect from the diversity of non-human forest life surrounding the cruisers' bodies. The proximity of the forest looms over the disaffected cruising site as a brooding backdrop of untapped potentiality for queer revival, reinvention and rewilding.

At the beginning of *Stranger*, the cruising site has become a place of mechanical efficiency rather than transgressive adventure. Organised across a period of ten discrete days, the film begins each day in roughly the same way, with static shots introducing us to the separate spaces of the cruising site: the carpark, the forest, the beach and the lake. The cruisers move between these spaces in a highly programmatic, codified manner. Kagan bullet-points the programme: 'Arrive, park, walk, undress, swim, cruise, fuck, repeat' (Kagan, 2013, p. 37). Friedman traces the men's paths around the site – from car park to forest to beach to lake to beach to forest, etc – as a living geometry that structures and activates the sexual encounters and '[provokes] characters to be read as abstract points and vectors' (Friedman, 2016, p. 183). Connor Winterton analyses this cruising cartography as a Foucauldian heterotopia, both open and closed, constructed of this 'system' of movements and gestures (Winterton, 2018, p. 53). This slick efficiency, however, initially evokes economic cycles rather than orgasmic pleasure. John Powers writes of the cruising site as a space in which the possibility of freedom is associated with a 'selfish lack of solidarity' (Powers, 2014), whilst Hugo Brown characterises the cruising beach as a metaphor for consumer society at large (Brown, 2013).

Indeed, a dialogue between Guiraudie and the filmmaker João Pedro Rodrigues sheds light on the cinematographic manipulation and sequencing of the supposedly natural spaces of the cruising lake and forest in *Stranger*. Rodrigues comments that Guiraudie 'rebuilt a natural space as if it were an architecture: using the mise en scène and the découpage' (Guiraudie & Rodrigues, 2013). Rodrigues further suggests Guiraudie's rhythming of the natural spaces of the film: 'there is a lot of wind and we hear the wind. We hear it frequently and we hear the cuts between the shots. It's as if there was a drive of nature in the story, a rhythm of nature in the story'. To this, Guiraudie replies: 'there is a rhythm, but there is also the architectural structure that you mentioned. The way to shoot up and down, the way to crop the space in small spaces in an architectonical way' (Guiraudie & Rodrigues, 2013).

Whilst Rodrigues' evocation of a 'drive of nature' suggests an element of agency proper to the physical environment, Guiraudie's insistence on the cinematographic *découpage* of the 'natural space' of the forest evokes the forest as a malleable raw material, passive to economic, cinematic and sexual appropriation. If for Simon Estok 'the commodification of nature and of sexual minorities are similar' (Estok, 2009, p. 214), Guiraudie's spatial appropriation of the natural environment at this point in the film dramatises parallel violences that turn bodies and landscapes into raw materials and objects of consumption. Guiraudie himself comments of the murderous character, Michel: 'Michel is a pleasure-seeker, a sexual consumer with a surfer's physique' (Frappat, 2013).

Indeed, I argue, if the forest later promises a rewilding of queer ecologies and modes of dwelling, the lake figures its opposite as a site of mechanistic dissolve and hygienic homogeneity. As the camera never glances below water, we experience the lake as a flat surface out of which bodies efficiently appear (Michel) or disappear (Michel's drowning of his first lover). Indeed, when we first see Michel's emergence from the lake, rather than the carpark, it is as if he is materialising directly from its liquids.

Within the cruising rotations between the beach, forest and lake that produce countless sexual encounters, the lake represents not only a platform for show and display (Franck is consistently impressed by Michel's swimming) but also figures a site at which each encounter or experience might be effectively washed off before beginning again, rinsing and repeating. The production line between lake and beach evokes the fast, industrialised 'clean bodies' of Kristin Ross's modernising, capitalist France (Ross, 1995).

Fig. 1: Image courtesy of Peccadillo Pictures.

Whereas fluids have dominated queer theory with the promise of dissolving hegemonic power structures – think the 'liquid flux of *jouissance*' (Žižek, 1989, p. 71) so beloved of Edelman's queer negativity or the 'flows of intensity' of a body without organs (Deleuze & Guattari, 2004, p. 179) – liquids in *Stranger* figure an eerie plane of hygiene or murder, cycling, recycling and disposing of compliant bodies.

Watching over this flat circulation of bodies, the figure of a disinterested masturbator returns throughout the film, walking around the cruising forest constantly in search of a couple or an orgy that he can watch whilst touching himself (Figure 1). This masturbator presents us with a hollow parody of queer *jouissance*; he appears oddly disengaged and indifferent to the live sex acts he is witnessing, and he is repeatedly thwarted in his attempts at orgasmic voyeurism by cruisers who tell him to leave. It is partly through this masturbator's ambivalent gaze that we see the forest early on in the film: as a site of mediocre pornography and flaccid desire. The masturbator encourages a point of identification for the film spectator's own gaze in the era of post-transgressive hypervisibility described by Rees-Roberts (Rees-Roberts, 2015, p. 139). The easily accessible images of naked bodies before us should be shocking or arousing, yet we remain in a maintained, ambivalent limbo, neither fully aroused nor fully disinterested by the penises, erect or soft, in front of us on screen. Even pornography theorist Linda Williams seems unsure of what to make of *Stranger*'s sex, placing the film in the middle-of-the-road category of *'relatively explicit'* (Williams, 2014, p. 16, original emphasis).

This erotic bathos is also tangible in a scene at the beginning of the film where Franck settles for having sex with someone he is not attracted to when he finds that Michel, the true object of his desires, is occupied with someone else. The sexual encounter between the two men begins with a discussion of sexual hygiene and precautionary measures. Franck attempts to perform oral sex on the man; however, the man refuses without a condom. The scene then cuts to the only unsimulated cum-shot in the entire film. Whilst Winterton argues that the close of the penis ejaculating '[concludes] the scene (giving it narrative purpose)' and 'represents the deep sexual fulfilment Franck is searching for' in a way that simultaneously mimics and subverts the traditional 'money shot' in pornography (2018, p. 59), I would emphasize that this cum-shot is characterised by a feeling of distance and disaffection precisely because it *does* recall the mechanisms, lack-luster performances and dodgy cuts of pornography. The quick cut to the penis self-consciously alerts us to the cinematographic artifice of the sequence, nodding to the use of a body double. The climax is reached via mechanical strain rather than the ecstatic approach of *jouissance*; Franck is masturbating himself, with minimal contact from the other man, who seems to be lying in wait, like a fluffer on a porn set. Further, Franck's instruction at the moment of his climax – 'kiss me!' – recalls less the exclamation of a passionate lover than a porn director's shouted stage directions. Lying side by side, the bodies are separate, individual, and protected, as if the absent condom is phantasmatically wrapped around the two bodies. If queer utopia is to be found in this forest, it is not here in this orgasm.

Guiraudie himself says: 'If sexual liberation leads to an obligation to come, it can quickly become alienating' (Frappat, 2013). The ejaculation is less an ecstatic cum-shot than a distant gaze of surveillance, which polices the liquid semen, making sure it arrives on cue and does not contaminate any body outside of Franck's. However, there is another moment of surveillance that precedes the sex, so quick that it is easily missed. Just before Franck's' anonymous encounter with the man, the camera turns to the forest floor, revealing the waste and detritus discarded by their fellow cruisers: discarded condoms, condom wrappers, boxes, tissues, etc (Figure 2). If, as Andil Gosine explains, surveillance in the media tracking gay men having sex in natural spaces has historically '[focused] on the litter and damage to the environment produced by homosexual acts' (Gosine, 2010, p. 158), pathologising queer bodies as dangerous pollutants, the camera's surveying of the detritus from above momentarily recalls the violence of this surveillance.

Franck, irritated, brushes away the detritus. However, despite Franck's hasty attempt to clear it, the rubbish largely stays put, exceeding the parameters of the frame and suggesting widescale littering throughout the forest. At stake here, I suggest, is not the environmental damage that the rubbish may or may not incur (indeed, the forest's vegetation seems to be flourishing regardless), but rather Franck's lack of interest in the forest's floor: it is just a convenient surface for fucking, with convenient plants for hiding. A simple connection is suggested here between the fading of queer *jouissance* and environmental disregard, both catalysed by the injunction to produce and consume, and evidenced in the synthetic objects of modernity's reproductive consumerism (ironic as the condoms may be as markers of this reproductivity).

Fig. 2: Image courtesy of Peccadillo Pictures.

However, if the sex and unsimulated ejaculation about to happen on this space fail to titillate us, perhaps it is the forest floor we should have been paying attention to and not the naked bodies. Whilst the detritus of plastic waste is symptomatic of consumerist cycles, the nondegradable forms also point to resistant materialities that live on despite this system as queer ecologies rather than economies. Jeffrey L. Meikle suggests that the production of synthetic plastics is bound up with a pragmatist desire to control the world around us, envisaging 'a malleable universe open to human influence' in which we could 'shape the stuff of existence at a fundamental chemical level [...] to mold from it objects and environments unknown to prior civilizations' (Meikle, 1995, p. 9). The discarded forms of the condoms and plastic wrappers on the forest floor, however, attest to plastic's falling short of this promise.

Instead, a world of queer fertility is suggested that refuses and exceeds human appropriation. If McCaffrey is interested in the way *Staying Vertical* is organised cinematographically around geometric lines that lead to queer relationalities in becoming entangled, non-linear and rhizomatic (McCaffrey, 2019), the forest undergrowth here is composed of nothing but grassy lines that overlap in all directions, as if sketching pathways and communications between the plastic objects like a root system.

Morton's agenda in *Ecology Without Nature* is to theorise how we must no longer '[put] something like Nature on a pedestal and [admire] it from afar' (Morton, 2007, p. 5) in a way that prevents us from thinking about humans and how their productions participate in ecology. Seymour's task in *Bad Environmentalism* is to think an environmentalism not characterised by the usual affects of 'guilt, shame, didacticism, prescriptiveness, sentimentality, reverence' but by 'dissident, often-denigrated affects and sensibilities' (Seymour, 2018, pp. 4, 6). Guiraudie's eclectic forest floor, I argue, demands we think queerness in relation to an irreverent 'ecology without nature' comprised of what Morton would call the 'mesh' of life forms, human and non-human (Morton, 2010b, p. 28).

Franck's brushing aside of the rubbish in order to complete a sexual act from which he will seem oddly disconnected demonstrates his lack of interest in the forest as environment at this point. When asked by his sex partner why he does not mind being watched by the masturbator, Franck replies: 'I don't pay attention' (*'moi, je fais pas attention'*). This lack of attention, as we have seen, encompasses Franck's relation to the forest's ecosystems, composed of both 'organic' vegetation and 'synthetic' waste.

The philosopher of science Isabelle Stengers argues that we must approach the current environmental crisis through an ethics of 'paying attention' (Stengers, 2015). Whereas capitalism works by exploiting the earth (Gaia) precisely through promoting 'the *right not to pay attention* [*faire attention*]' (59, original emphasis), ecological catastrophe demands that we initiate 'a reciprocal apprenticeship to the art of paying attention' as a mode of listening to Gaia's pain and responding to it (105). In *Stranger*'s short shots that allow the forest's being to inhabit the full frame without human interference, Guiraudie also poses environmental knowing as a challenge of attention. If we succeed in paying attention, as the forest seems to be encouraging Franck (and us) to do, we will notice new modes of queer ecological dwelling beyond the human.

Whilst the lake efficiently determines the fluid maintenance and hygienic disposal of bodies, we must *pay attention* to ways in which the forest is nondegradable, refusing to dissolve or to be made 'clean'. Writing in an afterword to *Plasticity at the Dusk of Writing* (2010) about link between plasticity and autobiography, Malabou juxtaposes fluidity (and its propensity for dissolution) with plasticity:

> Existence reveals itself as plasticity, as the very material of presence, as marble is the material of sculpture. It is capable of receiving any kind of form, but it

also has the power to give form to itself. Being the stuff of things, it has the power both to shape and to dissolve a particular facet of individuality. A lifetime always proceeds within the boundaries of a double excess: an excess of reification and an excess of fluidification. When identity tends toward reification, the congealing of form, one can become the victim of highly rigid frameworks whose temporal solidification produces the appearance of unmalleable substance. Plasticity situates itself in the middle of these two excesses. (81)

Whilst rigidity is bad, fluidification figures a similar (if opposite) violence for Malabou. Plasticity is the mode of being that demands that a 'lifetime' is neither fully petrified nor dissolved, but able to take form in a way that allows this form to remain open to mutation. We now turn our attention, then, to ways in which the forest is 'plastic', and create new forms of community between human, non-human, and inorganic lifeforms: how do we pay attention to the forest's plastic autobiography?

Rewilding Queer Ecologies

Whilst the forest seems vulnerable to appropriation, the wilderness maintains a resistant, plastic core that rejects this appropriation whilst remaining open to change and mutation. Brinkema also focuses on the interview between Guiraudie and Rodrigues in her own interrogation of the cinematic forest space. Whilst, as we saw, Guiraudie's comments imply the malleability of the forest before the camera's lens, Brinkema's own reading suggests that there is something in the cine-forest's architectonics that remains irreducible to human perception and order, thus refusing appropriation. Brinkema focuses on a discrepancy between what Guiraudie describes as 'scenographic' and Rodrigues describes as 'geometric'. For Brinkema, whilst Guiraudie's use of the term 'scenographic' in the interview describes construction of the sensuous landscape of the forest and the lake, Rodrigues' 'geometric' anticipates a strange preoccupation with measurements which runs throughout the film, most notably in a conspicuously precise discussion between the protagonists Franck and Henri as to how big the Silurus fish are that are said to inhabit the lake. Brinkema argues:

> While the scenographic figures what is composed and structured to be seen and felt, the geometric evacuates the 'what is seen and felt' – it is the generative making unknown of all of those dimensions. Landscape thereby remains l'inconnu. Instead of being located in the scenographic and all its attendant concepts (affect, atmosphere, allegory), horror is lodged within the question of the indifference of measurement itself. The film's most violent gesture is its spacing from the interpretability of the relation or relative positions of desire and violence. It emplaces horror in the uncompromising figure of measurability without meaning (Brinkema, 2018, p. 380).

In distinguishing between the scenographic and the geometric, Brinkema identifies a resistant core within the natural environment that encircles the cruisers, which is radically irreducible to any human or anthropomorphic usage or appropriation: this resistant core is nothing less than the 'brutal measurability' of the landscape, which remains utterly and hideously indifferent to conscious human intervention and constitutes the central horror of the film as a 'landscape-without-us model of horror' whereby alien exactitudes of measurement determine the (in)difference between life and death (Brinkema, 2018, p. 379).

Indeed, the inhuman indifference of the forest in *Stranger* does not have to signify pure horror, but also brings with it a glimmer of ecological hope. If there is something in the forest – some anarchical, environmental violence – that resists the architectonics of Guiraudie's cinematography or the efficient cycles of consumer sex, then there remains organic life and space within the forest that promises other modes of being or desiring. Whilst disaffected consumer sex spills its hygienic detritus across the forest floor, Brinkema's 'indifference' might also designate an ecological resistance to human intervention or pollution, as well as other, experimental interactions between organic vegetation and the synthetic materials of the condoms and wrappers on the forest's floor.

Heather Davis, for instance, explores new forms of nature that are anything but 'natural' in the traditional sense, showing how interactions between synthetic plastic materials and the microbial life sustained by them create a synthetic–organic hybrid landscape in which 'our plasticized, microbial progeny will offer a decidedly queerer world' (Davis, 2015, p. 246). If Walton argues that '[t]hrough its own stylistic ways of behaving, the film orients itself as being apart from human or environmental concerns, and detached from who or what the camera is engaged in observing' (Walton, 2018, p. 250), recalling Brinkema's analysis of the filmic landscape's alien immeasurability and the disaffected, cold plastic on the forest floor, I would counter that it is perhaps precisely through the camera's alignment with or collapsing into the withdrawal of the alien, biological landscape in Guiraudie's work that a queer environmental ethics is sparked.

If the ambivalent, disinterested masturbator suggests one point of identification for the viewer, a secondary identification with the forest itself is encouraged by shots that linger on the vegetation of the forest devoid of human interaction, or audio that records the unseen animal and insect life inhabiting the forest (this soundscape is brilliantly detailed in Walton, 2018). This identification with the forest is an identification with that ecology of alien, immeasurable geometries that Brinkema demonstrates to exceed and elude the body of the (queer) human. Indeed, certain shots align the forest with the cinematic apparatus itself, suggesting the forest as its own, organic mode of cinematic production anterior to and exterior to human moving image technology. Shots throughout the film fill the majority of the frame with leaves lit from behind by the sun, suggesting affinities between the organic surface of the leaf and thin sheets of celluloid passing through the camera or screens for projection (Figure 3). In other shots, the sun beams are passed through pinholes in the forest's canopy, connoting the apparatus of the camera obscura or the projector in a cinema (Figure 4).

As the sunbeam is coming towards the camera rather than away from it, it

Fig. 3: Image courtesy of Peccadillo Pictures.

Fig. 4: Image courtesy of Peccadillo Pictures.

is as if the forest itself is projecting on to us rather than vice versa, reversing the logic of photographic agency between object and image. The cine-forest reveals itself to be its own organic mode of image and narrative production that is entirely indifferent to the human narratives played against it, or Guiraudie's own 'architectonic', sculpting lens. Indeed, it may not be, as

Brinkema suggests, that the cine-forest's violence lies in its 'measurability without meaning' (Brinkema, 2018, p. 380) but precisely that the cine-forest is capable of generating its own meanings and cinemas that are radically unintelligible by the human. The 'landscape-without-us' (Brinkema, 2018, p. 379) forest's ecological violence, simultaneously the promise of its fertile self-cultivation, is precisely that it *means* without us. If Young locates *Stranger*'s queer resistance to appropriation in its mobilising 'some inscrutable negativity [which] interrupts the free flow of information, some terrifying opacity of the signifier' (Young, 2018, p. 237), the forest itself renders this opacity fertile with the promise of an ecologically vital *queerness-without-us*.

Thus, a plastic relation opens up between Guiraudie's human inhabitation and sculptural manipulation of the queer forest, and the forest's own pushing back against this cinematographic sculpting. The forest is not just a raw material to be consumed in efficient circuits of production but a resistant materiality but pushes back, throwing out forms, configurations and sounds utterly indifferent to the human projects within it. This two-way mutability evidences Malabou's instance that plasticity is both the capacity to receive form and to give form; or, as thought by the plastic cine-forest, to be projected and to project back. This mutual giving and receiving form between the queer forest and its sculpting by human inhabitation calls for the human protagonists and the filmic image itself to enter and to risk a more transgressive, ecological exposure to the forest.

This plastic give-and-take evokes Dana Luciano and Mel Y. Chen's investigations into 'queer inhumanisms' in which they are interested not in boundaryless fusions or dissolves between humans and non-humans but rather in tracing 'how those categories rub on, and against, each other, generating friction and leakage' (Luciano & Chen, 2015, p. 186). In this way, the queer, alien worlds of plants, animals, insects, corpses, plastic condom wrappers and boxes, telephone wires, helicopters, bodily excretions, and unidentifiable sounds and forms, figure queer materialities and inhuman ecologies to be explored, cultivated, allowed to grow wild, mutating (with and beyond) queer humans.

Chartering the queer landscapes left in the wake of the Anthropocene in ways which resonate with Morton's manifesto for an 'ecology without nature' and again recalling the organic-synthetic landfill of the forest floor, Davis delivers a manifesto for queer community and ethics of care beyond and after the human:

> Just as plastics are inadvertently creating all kinds of new worlds, such as the plastisphere, in order to address the current situation ethically, we must also learn to accept all kinds of strange life forms, human and nonhuman, toward which we generate care, compassion, and commitment. [...] We need to generate a sense of responsibility for our nonhuman progeny, these strange new forms of microbial life, while at the same time recognizing that their

existence is predicated on the extinguishment of multiple other forms of life: humans, animals, plants, and bacteria alike (Davis, 2015, p. 245).

The forest is asking for the viewer's sacrifice to its nonhuman indifference and ecological excess, in which it continues and flourishes as a mode of queer habitation and cinematic production beyond human life and narrative.

Indeed, the end of the film calls to us for total surrender and sacrifice to the unknown of the forest. Franck has just witnessed Michel murder both his friend Henri and the inspector, running off into the forest to hide and escape a similar fate. We see their dead and dying bodies disappearing into the undergrowth, swallowed by the forest. When the sun goes down, throwing the forest into darkness, Franck seems to have a change of heart, again pining for his murderous lover rather than fearing him, walking boldly into the dark of the forest, exposed to the unknown and to attack from all angles, calling Michel's name louder and louder. By this point, the forest has become too dark to properly make out any forms visually and we lose track of Franck's voice. We are left with nothing but the sounds of the forest, to which we now become hyperalert, forced suddenly to *pay attention*. The feeling is one of intense exposure: in the darkness; we do not know what direction we are facing, unable to orient ourselves in relation to the rigidly demarcated spatial architectonics of the forest.

If Guiraudie does indeed deliver us a Bataillean moment of self-shattering, orgasmic 'limit experience' here (Guiraudie often cites the influence of Georges Bataille on his work; see Aguilar, 2014) then I suggest that it is not, or at least not mainly, in the human sexual encounters that the cruising forest facilitates, or even Franck's sex with Michel, but precisely in Franck's self-sacrifice to the non-human, plastic ecologies within which he becomes willingly lost. Further, if Walton notes that *Stranger* becomes increasingly claustrophobic in its increased enclosure in the woods towards the film's climax (Walton, 2018, p. 259), this forest's approach encourages Franck's sacrifice spatially, removing the forest's exits. Within this enclosure, the film denies closure: we never know if Franck finds Michel, if he lives or dies. Unlike the conspicuously staged ejaculation, the film itself does not come but remains forever *still to come*. In this tempo-spatial suspension from which Franck cannot escape, he can only transform.

Malabou reminds us in *Plasticity at the Dusk of Writing* that plasticity describes a mode of metamorphosis provoked precisely by the impossibility of escape. A plastic form transforms at the moment of '[t]he impossibility of fleeing' when

> an extreme tension, a pain, a sensation of uneasiness surges toward an outside that does not exist. Something that is so constituted as to make fleeing impossible while also making it necessary to flee this impossibility. What is a 'way out'; what could a 'way out' be when there is not outside, no 'elsewhere'? It is not a question of how to escape closure but rather of how to escape within closure itself (2010, p. 65).

Further, '[t]he only possible solution to the impossibility of fleeing would thus be formation or transformation, that is to say, in the first place, the constitution of closure in a form that changes it into an equivalent of flight, by way of bypassing, avoiding, and displacing the prohibition of transition or transgression' (65–66). It is as if Malabou is present in Guiraudie's and Franck's twilight, forested *huis-clos* when she says: 'dusk is a time of metamorphosis' (Malabou, 2010, p. 61). Dusk is the time when forms are at their most plastic, when plasticity itself *comes*. As Guiraudie himself says: 'When the sun goes down, there are fascinating transformations, at that blue hour when all the birds start to sing' (Frappat, 2013).

The darkness and the swelling sounds of the final shot set the stage for a coming transformation. However, whilst Walton reads this moment as one of infinitely deferred event and 'embodied apprehension' (Walton, 2018, p. 260), I want to insist, with Malabou, that the impossibility of fleeing Guiraudie's dusk-lit forest beckons not annihilation but rather 'formation or transformation' out of the impossibility of escape. Through the heighted soundscape of the forest, we bear witness to the (trans)formation of a coming ecosystem of new lifeforms precisely in the (trans)formation and reordering of our audio-visual cinematic senses. The end of *Stranger* suggests that queer transgression, experience and *jouissance* will not be realised as an escaping nature or essence but precisely as a sacrificial exposure to the biological and the ecological, which activates the transformation of nature itself.

Walton urges her reader at the end of her analysis of *Stranger* that more work is needed on the 'corporeal gaps and spacings of cinema' that evidence 'the diversity of human, non-human and cinematic rhythms'. At this point, Walton's own analysis performatively follows *Stranger* and 'fades to black, accompanied by the sounds of an impervious wind and the night-time cries of cicadas' (Walton, 2018, p. 260). In search of the plastic forms of transformation inhabiting Guiraudie's forest at dusk – forms of 'human, non-human and cinematic rhythms', perhaps – we must cruise a few more of Guiraudie's queer forests.

The King of Escape is, fittingly, a film about a man's escape – or inability to escape – within the enclosure of the forest. Here, the forest beckons the human protagonists to give themselves to it but goes even further, inviting them to cultivate new, mystical forms of queer vegetation within it. As in *Stranger*, the cruising site at the beginning of *The King* evokes a disaffected efficiency: cars rotate around the carpark, maintaining a steady, if lethargic, production line of bodies, whilst Jean-Jacques talks to Armand about his tireless sexual conquests. The trees surrounding the frame hint at the presence of the neighboring forest as an opaque, inviting contrast to the performative visibility of the open carpark.

The promise of vegetal life intrudes upon the scene, however, when Jean-Jacques announces he has been consuming a 'doo-root' grown in the forest that gifts him superhuman libido. Jean-Jacques's usage of the doo-root recalls a fairly normative pharmaceutical usage like Viagra, with Jean-Jacques suggesting he uses it to have sex with people he is not attracted to. However, Armand discovers a more anarchic relationship with the root when he loses interest in the cruising carpark (which eventually gets shut down and blocked by bollards) and enters the forest.

Once in the forest, Armand spies the men of the town masturbating together having eaten the mysterious 'doo-root' and discovers a patch of earth on the forest floor where the root is being grown. After they have masturbated, Armand hears one man exclaim 'I'm still horny!' whilst the others list obligations that are pulling them back to the town and out of the woods. When the men are masturbating, their backs turned to the camera, they are seemingly not interacting with one another but facing the forest itself, as if directing their sexual energy towards the unspecified landscape of trees and plants. Here, the forest itself constitutes not a singular love object but an expansive, libidinous ecology.

Analysing Guiraudie's first and as-of-yet only novel *Now The Night Begins*, McCaffrey traces an '(im)personal relationality' in which homosexual desire fails to direct itself at any discrete, locatable object and instead becomes dispersed over places and planes. In one scene, the protagonist Gilles engages in 'undirected masturbation' at the house of his friends, Mariette and Pépé, confessing he is not thinking about them in particular but feels erotically comfortable in their home in general (McCaffrey, 2016, p. 62). McCaffrey argues that the non-directional flow of queer desire falls upon interchangeable objects, each representing the Lacanian *objet a*. Whilst the *objet a* is a polymorphous, phantasmatic love object – changing into whatever it wants, assuming any number of forms – the men's active cultivation of the doo-root in the forest suggests a symbiotic, organic transformability between the forest and the human bodies, which cultivates new forms of pleasure.

This eco-erotic desire for the forest is also enacted by Armand when he discovers the spot where the root is growing and eats some himself. He immediately sets off at a run, galloping through the forest. The previously-static camera angles become tracking shots, pivoting to follow Armand as he crashes through the undergrowth. In each shot, the camera pans to follow Armand before seemingly tiring of him, pausing to allow him to leave the frame and contemplate the forest devoid of the human body, if only for a fraction of a second (Figure 5). As *Stranger*'s long shots of vegetation unpopulated by humans in *Stranger by the Lake* attest, the forest exceeds and swallows its human inhabitants; their narratives are finite, fleeting happenings within the forest's greater ecology.

Whilst Nicole Seymour looks at tracking shots of the landscape in Ang Lee's *Brokeback Mountain* (2005) as mimicking a form of 'biosurveillance' of 'nature' which parallels the social, technological surveillance of the two queer protagonists (Seymour, 2013, p. 117), the camera here subverts the

Fig. 5: Image courtesy of Peccadillo Pictures.

logic of surveillance in becoming distracted by the forest and losing sight of Armand, enabling his escape whilst showing an underlying focus on vegetation to exceed interest in the human. The next time we see Armand, he is masturbating with his back turned to the camera (Figure 6); just like the men he was spying on, Armand's masturbation is an eco-erotic communion with the forest in its entirety rather than any one discrete object or body.

Rees-Roberts reads Armand's running through the forest through the work of the queer theorist Sara Ahmed on orientation and directionality; in following Armand's 'disorientating' pathways through the forest, the film 'visualizes some of the concerns articulated by queer theorist Sara Ahmed,

Fig. 6: Image courtesy of Peccadillo Pictures.

who has argued that queerness is not simply a question of identity and sexuality, but also one of orientation and affect' (Rees-Roberts, 2015, p. 452). Rees-Roberts argues, 'the film's formal emphasis on the direction of Armand's desire-path foregrounds the narrative's attempt to give shape to a personal crisis through an awareness of its topography' (ibid.). However, the tensions between stasis and movement, between Armand's fleeting form and the vegetal life that dominates the frame, suggests that these orientations give way to ecologies of desire: the constant movement and rotation of the cruising carpark is replaced by a transformed cruising of the forest predicated on careful cultivation and stops and starts rather than constant movement.

An inspector happens on Armand from behind, disallowing Armand's orgasm, shouting: 'You won't make any children that way!' The inspector's jibe suggests that Armand's crime is precisely his engagement with a type of sexuality that threatens the 'reproductive futurism' Edelman associates with heteronormative economy (Edelman, 2004, p. 26). Reprimanding Armand for his involvement with a young woman from the village, the inspector then states that 'little girls belong with their fathers', further equating this reproductive futurity with the reproduction of the patriarchal genealogies. Edelman, then, would no doubt celebrate Armand's eco-erotic desire for the forest as powerfully queer in its anti-Child negativity.

The inspector's accusation of reproductive impotence, however, is undermined by the fervent green diversity filling the frame behind the naked figure of Armand. Whilst Armand's eco-erotica may be non-reproductive in human terms, the forest presents us with an image of all-encompassing non-human fertility, from the wet mud beneath Armand's feet (which acts as a sludgy parody of the hygienic dissolve of *Stranger*'s lake) to the rich diversity of green plant life and the sounds of animals that mix with Armand's own panting. Whilst the vegetation maintains the opacity that Young celebrates in Guiraudie's work, this opacity itself evokes the 'plasticity of vegetal sexuality' (Marder, 2016, p. 115) in its intricate, interconnected diversity. Again, Guiraudie's cine-forest invites new cross-fertilisations of queer desire not in opposition to nature but precisely in relation to a nature imaged as a canopy of diverse plasticities between human and non-human life forms.

Storytellers of the Queer Forest

Whilst the forest might indeed exceed human life and narrative, Guiraudie's filmic forests privilege modes of storytelling that are attributable neither to autonomous human subjects nor to the forest's own mysterious cinemas, figuring instead a plastic interplay of queer communications and *expressions* between the two. Indeed, Guiraudie's queer forests are bursting with and sustained by stories, myths and oral histories, from the myth of the 'second to last sleep' that catalyses Basile's wandering in *No Rest for the Brave*, to the rumored monster fish in *Stranger by the Lake*.

Staying Vertical, in particular, foregrounds questions of narrative and storytelling in relation to the forest's ecologies and biologies. The protagonist, Léo, is a screenwriter with writer's block who is traveling through the countryside in search of inspiration. Like most of Guiraudie's protagonists, he is a queer wanderer who spends the film in a nomadic state of passage through forests, fields and plateaus. Léo begins a relationship with a shepherdess, with whom he fathers two children; however, he finds himself more entangled in desiring relations with the men of the village. Léo's story – the screenplay that he is struggling to write – becomes bound up with the forest. The forest is somewhere Léo escapes to when he is in need of inspiration; it is also a site in which he hides and escapes his editor who is always chasing him for his latest draft. The forest, therefore, figures a site of intersection between Léo's queer storytelling and his interconnection with the biological and ecological (trans)formations of the forest.

The biological freedom articulated in Malabou's plasticity becomes associated with a certain kind of storytelling, from the autobiographical self which emerges precariously between rigidity and fluidity as we saw (Malabou, 2010, p. 81), to forces of gene 'expression' or 'interpretation' as described by epigenetics: organisms develop more like open-ended, performatively embellished stories than predetermined blueprints. In *Before Tomorrow*, Malabou turns from (neuro)plasticity to epigenetics more broadly (of which neuroplasticity is one particular example). Epigenesis is the study of how organic life forms develop by *expressing* or *interpreting* gene sequences, rather than by adhering to them perfectly. Referring to the oft-cited metaphor in science that epigenetics is like giving the same book (DNA) to many different readers (gene interpretation or expression of this DNA), Malabou argues: 'The image of interpretation, whether textual or musical, evokes the style, individual fashioning, and endless possibilities for reading or playing in every instance. The use of this image does seem to indicate the opening of a hermeneutic dimension in the heart of the biological' (Malabou, 2016, p. 89). Further:

> If epigenetic factors encompass physical mechanisms as much as environmental and social influences, then how, in the constitution of phenotypical individuality, could this be anything but the formation of a singularity that transcends strict determinism and places epigenesis and the development of all living beings in an intermediary space between *biology* and *history*? (ibid., original emphasis).

If the 'essence' despised by queer theory rests on 'a total philosophical ignorance of the meaning of the word "essence"' (Malabou, 2011, p. 136), Malabou's fertilisation of philosophy with molecular biology demonstrates that essence is innately epigenetic: biological essence, free to express and interpret itself, tells stories that constantly uproot and transform the nature of this essence. Christopher Watkin explores further the narrative implications of Malabou's epigenetic hermeneutics, likening the epigenesis of an organism to Paul Ricœur's account of selfhood as narrative whereby an epigenetic self is constituted of stories that are '(1) non-originary, (2) collaborative, (3) tensive, and (4) never definitive' (Watkin, 2017, p. 136).

Once in the forest, Léo arrives at the mysterious house of a woman living amongst the trees. The woman seems to be a kind of healer or therapist whose work consists in putting her patients' bodies in communion with the forest. The healer connects Léo to the leaves of the tree. The branches and vines of the tree connect to Léo in the same way that tubes and wires might connect to a patient in a hospital, or electrodes might be attached to the heart or the brain in order to obtain diagnostic or experimental readings (Figure 7). The healer asks Léo questions, invoking a typical scene of the psychoanalytic transference in which the patient lies on a couch and talks to the psychoanalyst behind them. McCaffrey has noted the ways in which this scene parodies psychoanalysis precisely through the tree, recalling the Deleuzo–Guattarian deconstruction of psychoanalysis via the model of the rhizome (McCaffrey, 2019).

Indeed, if the scene pokes fun at psychoanalysis, it also pokes fun at Edelman's brand of queer negativity, which takes as its central motor the cornerstone of Freudian psychoanalysis: the death drive. Further, whilst psychoanalysis traditionally uses a patient's self-narratives to access a discrete, located psychic trauma, Watkin's Ricœurian account of epigenetic storytelling as being without origin and forever unfinished renders the psychoanalytic genealogy unfeasible. The *destructive* negativity of psychoanalysis's death drive, then, is attached to the *constructive* plasticity of organic life through the vines connecting Léo to the tree. Michael Washington has suggested the potential for Malabou's plasticity to rethink queer negativity, yoking the possibility of formation to queer negativity, citing the unexpected register of biological fertility suggested by Marquis de Sade when Sade says that '[w]ithout destruction the earth would receive no nourishment' (Washington, 2018, p. 212).

Edelman's anti-futurity adamantly rallies against narrative; narrative constitutes the structure of the fantasy image of reproductive futurity, creating 'history as linear narrative (the poor man's teleology) in which meaning succeeds in revealing itself – *as itself* – through time' (Edelman, 2004, p. 4). Futurity's narrative production of heteronormative temporality is further attached on to nature through fictions of natural cycles and seasonal rotations, which act to naturalise narrative (57–58). In Guiraudie's films, seen here with Léo, it is precisely the opposite: it is not that narrative imposes itself on nature in a malign agenda to naturalise the hegemonic Symbolic order, but precisely that nature itself becomes an anarchic organic ecology that produces stories that undo and queer those promoted by the Symbolic.

Stories, as Edelman fears, may indeed be innately yoked to the biological

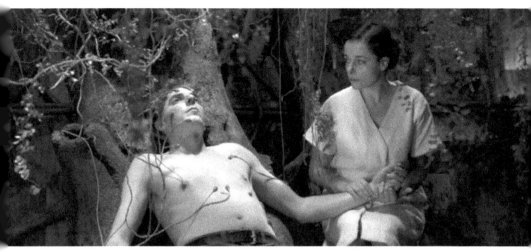

Fig. 7: Image courtesy of Peccadillo Pictures.

and the ecological; however, as Malabou's epigenetic hermeneutics shows, this does not mean there has to be anything innately normative about either biology or narrative. Stories and narratives become a mechanism of biology's hermeneutic self-invention, rather than a transcendent narrative of control imposed on organisms from the outside. Léo's open-ended storytelling evokes Malabou's characterisation of epigenetic development in organisms as a necessarily unfinished, unpredictable and undetermined hermeneutics. Edelman misunderstands 'narrative' just as queer theory misunderstands 'essence'.

This forest setting is intimately connected with Léo's compulsions as a storyteller. In one scene, Léo escapes from his editor's demands in the forest. When the editor tracks him down, demanding a draft of the screenplay, Léo locks himself within the healer's house, managing to produce much of his script overnight. Despite his editor's satisfaction, the healer offers Léo a chance to escape before he writes more, fearing his writing will become too prescribed and inauthentic. The forest, then, is both a catalyst for Léo's rapid production of writing and the demand never quite to be done with this writing, for this writing to avoid capture, for the interpretation and herme-neutics of the text always to stray, and to begin inventing new narratives before old narratives have fully settled.

Malabou's writing on epigenetics, and the hermeneutic (hi)stories epigenet-ics implies, organically evolves beyond the individual organism into a thinking of ecology or rather the ecological intersections between a network of different plasticities. Florence Chiew argues that Malabou's plastic brain must be thought in terms of its interconnectedness with wider ecologies rather than singularly to avoid a reading in which agency must come from 'elsewhere' (Chiew, 2012, pp. 52–53). Meanwhile, Watkin explicitly connects hermeneutics, organic plasticity and ecology in order to think Malabou's account of neural identity as 'eco-synaptic epigenesis' in which the singular self is constructed plastically through the organic–hermeneutic relations between multiple brains (Watkin, 2017, pp. 131–140). Malabou's plasticity, then, allows us to think new forms of queerness that are able to take form and change form, existing in connection with 'other plasticities' or 'other plastic forms of life' via the epigenetic strands of non-human hermeneutics and narratives.

At the end of *The King*, Armand escapes again into the forest to find the townsmen at it in the bushes. A well-endowed old man – a mythical figure among the cruising community of gay men throughout the film – tells Armand to go into the hut with him and Armand performs oral sex on him. The man asks Armand to stop before he orgasms and goes on to explain why in relation to his life story. The old man tells his life as an endless chain of lovers and personal transformations. His ability to have so many lovers, he claims, has to do with his not coming: 'as long as I do not come, I can continue to love'. Whilst Edelman's atemporal *jouissance* suggests a destruction of teleological hetero-reproductive temporality, so does the old man's complete occlusion of orgasm: the negation of orgasm enables an unbroken energy that entails the formation of community as an interconnected ecology of desire, in which the sexual act circulates rather than taking on a linear, teleological pathway. However, the old man's lack of orgasm does not simply result in another form of 'no future' as an ongoing stuck time, but rather opens him out to further metamorphoses.

The old man's retelling of his own sexual history foregrounds an oral tradition, a narrative mode enfleshed and eroticised by Armand's performing oral sex on him just before he tells his life story. The open-endedness of his story reflects its contents: that of the eternally delayed orgasm. The other men of the town enter the cabin made of wood from the forest and join Armand and the old man, turning off the light to go to sleep; as with the cut to black at the end of *Stranger*, the soundscape of the forest is the last thing to go. We hear the men rustling around in the cabin, encompassed by the vital buzzing quiet of the forest at night as the credits begin to roll. Orgasm is substituted for organism in Guiraudie's queer forest.

Here, we are presented with a modest queer utopia. The cozy cabin in the woods is a dwelling of neither self-shattering transgression nor dystopian non-futurity, but rather the quiet potentiality of a queer cultivation of hermeneutic and epigenetic interactions with non-human surroundings (Figures 8–9). The queer cabin here does not equal the efficient appropriation of the forest's topography at work at the beginning of *Stranger*, but rather constructs an almost imperceptible dwelling of queer cultivation that, fragile and modest, exists at the threshold of disappearance into the forest.

Whether his cine-forests end in destruction or construction, murder or orgy, Guiraudie's eco-systems reveal essence to be plastic and epigenetic; 'nature'

Fig. 8: Image courtesy of Peccadillo Pictures.

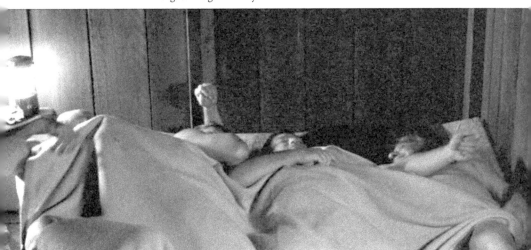

Fig. 9: Image courtesy of Peccadillo Pictures.

reclaims its queerness in an expression of biology's own plea for metamorphosis and mutation. Nurturing and nourishing nature's mutations, Guiraudie's forests are plastic ecologies in which queer subjectivities, singularities and communities are permitted to take tentative *form* precisely at the point of dissolution, precisely in the cultivation of stories that negotiate forms of queer being between human, animal, insect, plant and rock life. Thus, for Guiraudie, it is an environmental, ecological, geological, biological imperative to listen and *pay attention* to the stories produced and cultivated by queer bodies and communities. Somewhere in the queer forest a new, mutant relation to our world is being both grown and left to grow wild.

References

Aguilar, C. & Guiraudie, A. (2014), 'Interview: Alain Guiraudie on his Alluring and Explicit Film "Stranger by the Lake"', *Indiewire*, 20 February [online], https://www.indiewire.com/2014/02/interview-alain-guiraudie-on-his-alluring-and-explicit-film-stranger-by-the-lake-168913/ (accessed 9 October 2018).

Ahmed, S. (2006), *Queer Phenomenology: Orientations, Objects, Others*, Durham: Duke University Press.

Brinkema, E. (2018), 'Strangers by Lakes: 1 or 2 or 4 or 5 or 10', *Discourse*, Vol. 40, No. 3, pp. 370–381.

Brown, H. (2013), '"L'inconnu du lac", un film de Alain Guiraudie', *Hugobrown.net*, 13 June [online], http://www.hugobrown.net/article-l-inconnu-du-lac-un-film-de-alain-guiraudie-118473665.html (accessed 27 September 2018).

Brown, J. (2015), 'Being Cellular: Race, the Inhuman, and the Plasticity of Life', *GLQ: A Journal of Lesbian and Gay Studies*, vol. 21, no. 2–3, pp. 321–341.

Chiew, F. (2012), 'Neuroplasticity as an Ecology of Mind: A Conversation with Gregory Bateson and Catherine Malabou', *Journal of Consciousness Studies*, Vol. 19, No. 11–12, pp. 32–54.

Davis, H. (2015), 'Toxic Progeny: The Plastisphere and Other Queer Futures', *philoSOPHIA: A Journal of Continental Feminism*, Vol. 5, No. 2, pp. 231–250.

Deleuze, G., & Guattari, F. (2004), *A Thousand Plateaus*, London & New York: Continuum.

Di Chiro, G. (2010), 'Polluted Politics? Confronting Toxic Discourse, Sex Panic, and Eco-Normativity', in C. Mortimer-Sandilands & B. Erickson (eds), *Queer Ecologies: Sex, Nature, Politics, Desire*, Bloomington: Indiana University Press, pp. 199–230.

Edelman, L. (2004), *No Future: Queer Theory and the Death Drive*, Durham: Duke University Press.

Estok, S. (2009), 'Theorizing in a Space of Ambivalent Openness: Ecocriticism and Ecophobia', *ISLE: Interdisciplinary Studies in Literature and Environment*, Vol. 16, No. 2, pp. 203–225.

Frappat, H. (2013), 'Interview with Alain Guiraudie' [press release], https://medias.unifrance.org/medias/40/144/102440/presse/l-inconnu-du-lac-dossier-de-presse-anglais.pdf (accessed 21 January 2019).

Friedman, N. (2016), 'Diagram of the Amorous Search: Generating Desire with Guiraudie's *L'inconnu du lac*', *Scapegoat: Landscape, Architecture, Political Economy*, Vol. 9, pp. 183–188.

Garrard, G. (2010), 'How Queer is Green?', *Configurations*, Vol. 18, No. 1–2, pp. 73–96.

Gosine, A. (2010), 'Non-white Reproduction and Same-Sex Eroticism: Queer Acts Against Nature', in C. Mortimer-Sandilands & B. Erickson (eds), *Queer Ecologies: Sex, Nature, Politics, Desire*, Bloomington: Indiana University Press, pp. 149–172.

Guiraudie, A. (2018), *Now The Night Begins*, Los Angeles: Semiotext(e).

Guiraudie, A. & Rodrigues, J.P. (2013), 'Sex, Death, and Geometry: A Conversation Between Alain Guiraudie and João Pedro Rodrigues on *L'inconnu du lac*', *Cinema Scope*, No. 55, pp. 33–37.

Halberstam, J. and Nyong'o, T. (2018), 'Introduction: Theory in the Wild', *South Atlantic Quarterly*, Vol. 117, No. 3, pp. 453–464.

Hird, M.J. (2004), 'Naturally Queer', *Feminist Theory*, Vol. 5, No. 1, 85–89.

Kagan, D. (2013), '*Stranger by the Lake*', *Australian Book Review*, vol. 357, p. 37.

Kermabon, J. (2013). '*L'inconnu du lac* d'Alain Guiraudie', *24 images*, vol. 164, p. 10.

Loiselle, M-C. (2002), 'Que reste-t-il de nos labeurs? / Ce vieux rêve qui bouge d'Alain Guiraudie', *24 images*, vol. 111, p.16.

Luciano, D. & Chen, M.Y. (2015), 'Has the Queer Ever Been Human?', *GLQ: A Journal of Lesbian and Gay Studies*, Vol. 21, No. 2–3, pp. 183–207.

Malabou, C. (2008), *What Should We Do With Our Brain?*, New York: Fordham University Press.

Malabou, C. (2010), *Plasticity at the Dusk of Writing: Dialectic, Destruction, Deconstruction*, New York & Chichester: Columbia University Press.

Malabou, C. (2011), *Changing Difference: The Feminine and the Question of Philosophy*, Cambridge: Polity Press.

Malabou, C. (2016), *Before Tomorrow: Epigenesis and Rationality*, Cambridge: Polity Press.

Malabou, C. (2019), *Morphing Intelligence: From IQ Measurement to Artificial Brains*, New York: Columbia University Press.

Marder, M. & Irigaray, L. (2016), *Through Vegetal Being: Two Philosophical Perspectives*, New York & Chichester: Columbia University Press.

McCaffrey, E. (2016), '(Im)personal Relationality in Alain Guiraudie's *Ici commence la nuit*', *Revue Critique de Fixxion Française Contemporaine*, No. 12, pp. 60–71.

McCaffrey, E. (2019), 'Lupine and Zigzag Lines: Queer Affect in Alain Guiraudie's Cinema', *Contemporary French Civilization*, Vol. 44, No. 4. Forthcoming.

Meikle, J.L. (1995), *American Plastic: A Cultural History*. New Brunswick: Rutgers University Press.

Moffat, W. (2015), 'The Narrative Case for Queer Biography', in Warhol, R. & S.S. Lander (eds), *Narrative Theory Unbound: Queer and Feminist Interventions*, Columbus: Ohio State University Press, pp. 210–226.

Mortimer-Sandilands, C. & Erickson, B. (eds) (2010), *Queer Ecologies: Sex, Nature, Politics, Desire*, Bloomington: Indiana University Press.

Morton, T. (2007), *Ecology Without Nature: Rethinking Environmental Aesthetics*, Cambridge & London: Harvard University Press.

Morton, T. (2010a), 'Guest Column: Queer Ecology', *PMLA* Vol. 125, No. 2, pp. 273–282.

Morton, T. (2010b), *The Ecological Thought*, Cambridge & London: Harvard University Press.

Muñoz, J.E. (2009), *Cruising Utopia: The Then and There of Queer Futurity*, New York & London: New York University Press.

Powers, J. (2014), 'The Art of Cruising in *Gloria* and *Stranger by the Lake*', *Vogue*, 24 January [online], http://www.vogue.com/article/the-art-of-cruising-in-gloria-and-stranger-by-the-lake-movies (accessed 27 September 2018).

Rees-Roberts, N. (2015), '*Hors milieu*: Queer and Beyond", in A. Fox, M. Marie, R. Moine & H. Radner (eds), *A Companion to Contemporary French Cinema*, Chichester: Wiley Blackwell, pp. 439–460.

Ross, K. (1995), *Fast Cars, Clean Bodies: Decolonization and the Reordering of French Culture*, Cambridge: The MIT Press.

Roy, A. (2013). 'Tout est normal, tout est terminé: *L'inconnu du lac* d'Alain Guiraudie', *24 images*, Vol. 165, pp. 60–61.

Seymour, N. (2013), *Strange Natures: Futurity, Empathy, and the Queer Ecological Imagination*, Urbana: University of Illinois Press.

Seymour, N. (2018), *Bad Environmentalism: Irony and Irreverence in the Ecological Age*, Minneapolis: University of Minnesota Press.

Stengers, I. (2015), *In Catastrophic Times: Resisting the Coming Barbarism*, trans. by Andrew Goffey, London: Open Humanities Press.

Walton, S. (2018), 'Cruising The Unknown: Film as Rhythm and Embodied Apprehension in *L'Inconnu du lac/Stranger by the Lake* (2013)', *New Review of Film and Television Studies*, Vol. 16, No. 3, pp. 238–263.

Washington, M. (2017), *Giving an Account of the Queer Subject: Plasticity, Psychoanalysis, and Queer Theory*, Dissertation, Kingston University.

Washington, M. (2018), 'Reading Derrida's *Glas*: A Queer Presence alongside Hegel', in T. Wormald & I. Dahms (eds), *Thinking Catherine Malabou: Passionate Detachments*, London: Rowman & Littlefield International, pp. 201–217.

Watkin, C. (2017), *French Philosophy Today: New Figures of the Human in Badiou, Meillassoux, Malabou, Serres and Latour*, Edinburgh: Edinburgh University Press.

Williams, L. (2014), 'Cinema's Sex Acts', *Film Quarterly*, Vol. 67, No. 4, pp. 9–25.

Winterton, C. (2018), 'Blurred Lines: The Case of Stranger by the Lake', in L. Coleman & C. Siegel (eds), *Intercourse in Television and Film: The Presentation of Explicit Sex Acts*, Lanham: Lexington Books, pp. 43–65.

Young, D.R. (2018), *Making Sex Public and Other Cinematic Fantasies*, Durham: Duke University Press.

Žižek, S. (1989), *The Sublime Object of Ideology*, London: Verso.

Filmography

No Rest for the Brave (Alain Guiraudie, 2003).

The King of Escape (Alain Guiraudie, 2009).

Stranger by the Lake (Alain Guiraudie, 2013).

Staying Vertical (Alain Guiraudie, 2016).

Chapter 6

The 'Good' and 'Bad' Forests of Modern Fantasy Cinema: A Kleinian Topology

Alexander Sergeant

T he history of popular fantasy fiction is littered with forests. Co-opting iconographies of the European fairy tale, the fantasy genre has repeatedly turned to the atmospheric realm of the forest as the sources of much of its dreams, nightmares and otherwise outlandish scenarios. Snow White escaped to the woods, Red Riding Hood travelled through the woods, and Hansel and Gretel were abandoned in the woods. In a similar vein, fantasy forests often serve as key locus points of action and spectacle within popular Hollywood cinema produced over the last two decades, with franchises such as *Harry Potter* (2001–2011), *The Lord of the Rings* (2001–2003) and *The Hunger Games* (2012–2015) all gravitating to the forest as the key place to reveal their narrative mysteries, generate suspense and build their worlds on screen.

Yet, despite the forest's ubiquity within mainstream fantasy cinema, it is rarely considered as a source of study in its own right within the emerging scholarly discourses of the Hollywood fantasy film. Frances Pheasant-Kelly includes passing reference to the forests of *Harry Potter* and *The Lord of the Rings* in her consideration of how the imagery of post-9/11 fantasy films tap into prevalent cultural anxieties, offering up thoughts on how the forest provides opportunities for 'dark, sublime imagery' and/or instances of spatial terror (2013, pp. 48, 53). Similar asides to the function of forest are also provided by James Walters, Jacqueline Furby and Claire Hines in their respective case studies of fantasy cinema (see Walters, 2011, p. 123; Furby & Hines, 2011, p. 92). However, whilst forests are often briefly considered as part of the wider analysis of fantasy theorists and historians, the overall dramatic function or effect of forest imagery within fantasy cinema has yet to be considered.

This chapter seeks to offer an understanding of the function of forests within contemporary Hollywood fantasy cinema. It looks beyond the specifics of individual forests in fantasy films to consider the recurring traits that might offer some tentative conclusion as to why the forest has functioned and continues to function as a sight of fascination for both fantasy creators and audiences alike. To do this, I turn to a critical methodology that has enjoyed a historic and productive relationship with fantasy fiction, namely psycho-analysis. Both emerging out of the same cultural 'enquiry beyond empiri-cism' (Harris, 2008), fairy tales and psychoanalysis both sought to look beyond rationality and find meaning in dreamscapes, wonderlands and fantasy scenarios.

To argue for the continued relevance of psychoanalytic theory, this chapter considers the setting of the forest through an alternative psychoanalytic lens, namely that of the object relations theory of Melanie Klein. Expressed most directly in Klein's duality of the mother's 'good' and 'bad' breasts, early forms of object relations dependent upon phantasy are used to expose primordial anxieties and pleasures within the subject without recourse to logic or rationality that manifest throughout everyday life. Applying these 'good' or 'bad' relationships to recent examples of fantasy cinema, this chapter performs an exploratory, cross-textual analysis of different forests within fantasy filmmaking of the last two decades, utilising a Kleinian perspective to articulate the rich imaginative depths that lie beneath the image of the forest within contemporary popular culture.

Sometimes a Forest is not a Cigar:
The (Further) Uses of Enchantment

A popular but apocryphal anecdote recounts a story in which Sigmund Freud – founder of psychoanalysis – once commented that 'sometimes a cigar is just cigar' (Elms; 2001). This quotation is often used as the basis for the popular counterargument against the perceived dangers of psychoana-lytic interpretation, namely its tendency to prescribe on to the world hidden meanings through allusion to an abstracting set of psychic principles and tendencies. Once the dominant theoretical approach to film and media scholarship, psychoanalysis has been heavily critiqued by both cognitive and phenomenological theorists over the last two decades (see Bordwell, 1996, pp. 3–36; Sobchack, 1992, pp. 14–25).

Todd McGowan and Ben Tyrer have previously offered robust defences against such claims and, whilst there is not the space within this chapter to mount a lengthy defence of psychoanalysis against these accusations, the ideas already offered by such neo-Lacanian theorists showcase the contin-ued vibrancy and utility of psychoanalysis as both an investigative and interpretative tool (McGowan, 2003; Tyrer, 2016). Psychoanalysis teaches us that cigars are never *just* cigars. This does not mean they are not also cigars (objects used rationally and experienced sensually). However, like all objects encountered within the sphere of conscious meaning, a cigar becomes a cigar only through the way its objective characteristics are psychically fused to an individual's subjective experience.

This is why cigars mean different things to different people, whilst also allowing them to mean something to everybody. It is doubtful Freud ever said that a cigar is just a cigar. He did, however, state in his *New Introductory Lectures to Psychoanalysis* that dreams are 'not a means of giving information' (1933, p. 9). Unlike words, dream images are not symbols designed to communicate a fixed meaning and they do not operate as part of a lexicon shared across individuals. The point of interpretation in analysis within most schools of psychoanalysis is therefore not to prescribe a meaning on to a subject's subjective experience but to provide them with the means of articulating meaning for themselves through an intersubjective dialogue between analyst and analysand. It is to turn profound melancholia, anger, trauma or dreams into language so that they may be considered within the conscious realm.

Like dream images, it is often doubtful the forests of recent fantasy cinema are created within any clear symbolic meaning. They do not exist to be interpreted as rigid allegories or fixed metaphors. Such certainty of meaning would obfuscate the pleasures and purposes of interpretation when encountering narrative. However, like cigars, forests are not just forests. Different forests mean different things to different people; and different forests mean differently.

Unfortunately, the legacy of the application of Freudian theory in relation to discussions of fantasy do not always allow for the celebration of the diversity of meaning available to audiences thanks to the similarities between their narratives and dreams. Instead, psychoanalytic interpretation has often chosen to rationalise this dream-like imagery through a process of psychoanalytic decoding. Perhaps the most famous example of this psychoanalytic approach appears in Bruno Bettelheim's *The Uses of Enchantment*. In this classic defence of the fairy tale from accusations of triviality and banality due to their fantastical subject matter, child psychologist Bettelheim sought to demonstrate the important therapeutic value of such tales for precisely the same reasons. As Bettelheim argues:

> Fairy tales do not pretend to describe the world as it is, nor do they advise what one ought to do... The unrealistic nature of these tales (which narrow-minded rationalists object to) is an important device, because it makes obvious that the fairy tales' concern is not useful information about the external world, but the inner processes taking place in an individual (25).

For Bettelheim, the lack of objective truth presented within the fairy tale – not just presenting itself as a fictional version of reality but a fiction that transcends reality altogether – gives licence to the reader to seek meaning in the stories through their ability to speak to their emotional as opposed to factual sense of truth. Readers can use the stories as a means of processing deeply complex emotions and paradoxes that the subject is forced to reconcile with as part of the process of living in the world. Bettelheim advocates that those informed by psychoanalysis can use Freudian methods of dream analysis to articulate the likely effect of such stories, revealing their hidden psychic meaning beneath their subject matter. Bettelheim performs a number of readings of well-known fairy-tales, including 'Hansel and Gretel', 'Little Red Riding Hood' and 'Snow White' (159–165, 166–182, 199–214).

Within Bettelheim's analysis, the recurrent image of the forest contained within fairy tales is therefore considered sporadically as an environment of repressed sexuality. As he argues, 'since ancient times the near-impenetrable forest in which we get lost has symbolized the dark, hidden, near-impenetrable world of our unconscious' (94). This equation of the substance of the fairy tale with the realm of the unconscious is engrained within Bettelheim's wider methodology of the fairy tale as an expression of psychic reality over objective reality, offering little further insights into what the forest's specific function to the tale is beyond a single other reference to the mysterious qualities of the wood contained within his analysis of 'The Three Bears' (217).

Contextualised within Bettelheim's alternative readings of fairy tales, this allusion to the unconscious takes on a distinctly sexualised identity. This paradigm of the forest as womb, or at the very least, the forest as female sexuality, continues in other psychoanalytic interpretations of the function of the fictitious forest. In relation to a different cultural context entirely, Gillian Gillison repeats this conflation of the forest as a symbol for the vagina in her reading of the Gimi folklore of New Guinea (1994, p. 217). Within the world of theatre studies, Allen Dunn's analysis of William Shakespeare's *A Midsummer Night's Dream* draws from a popular interpretation of the play to argue that the forest environment into which the lovers escape from Thebes allows to play to explore its latent sexual content (1988).

In relation to cinema, Jack Zipes applies a similar Freudian analysis of the forest in his discussion of Neil Jordan's (1984) adaptation of Angela Carter's own revisionist take on the Red Riding Hood stories, *A Company of Wolves*. Zipes observes that the forest environment serves as a realm of fervent sexuality that gives its connotative associations with wildness and fertility, describing Jordan's depiction of the woods as a realm that 'pulsates with phallic snakes and womb-like wells and fertile eggs' (2011, p. 150). Once again, this particular forest is assigned a meaning much like all the other forests encountered, whether taken from different cultures, different times or different media examples.

Whilst I do not wish to contest the validity of these individual interpretations of specific examples of fairy tales, I would contest any attempt to extrapolate any abiding rule or principle from this persistent tendency to read the forest as a representation of female sexuality and fertility. It seems both intellectually and instinctively unsatisfying to do so, given the multi-faceted ways in which forests seem to exist within popular fantasy cinema and the resonance they achieve by being so many different things. Psychoanalysis always looks for underlying structures and principles behind individual appearances. However, those structures must be suitably malleable so as not to impose or replace a latent meaning on to the manifest content without acknowledging its nuance, its individuality and its richness as an appearance. The forest is too rich an entity within fantasy cinema to be contained by a single meaning. Instead, we need a topology of its capacities for different meanings.

To provide such a topology, I turn to the work of psychoanalyst Melanie Klein as a potential corrective to the quasi-insistence on sexualisation of dream imagery contained with post-Freudian analyses of the forest. I am by no means the first theorist to include Kleinian theories as part of an attempt to theorise the psychic underbelly of fantasy imagery. Bettelheim himself shows awareness of some of Klein's key concepts (namely the notion of the good and bad mother) in his theorisation of the recurrent figure of the wicked stepmother, whilst Carol Creed's 'monstrous-feminine' is indebted to Julia Kristeva's theoretical conceptualisation of the abject, which itself is informed by Klein's theories of early object relations (1993). Klein's theories have proven an important part of an attempt to theorise fantasy fiction precisely because of the emphasis she gives to the parts of the psyche that this mode of storytelling seems to speak most acutely towards, namely our capacity to imagine beyond our being. For Klein, 'phantasy begins at birth and never stops. External events always dance with phantasies and their partnership eventuates in the reported experiences and nonverbal expressions of the patient' (Solomon, 1995, p. 10).

In specific relation to the forest, Klein displays a number of fleeting instances of engagement with forest imagery in both her theoretical papers and clinical reports. In her analysis of Little Fritz, we see reports on her patient requesting his parents construct him a forest of Christmas trees, an act which Klein argues seemed to stem from his own desire to test their assumed omnipotence due to the assumptions of early infant Oedipal relations (1921, p. 14). Fritz's invocation of the forest seems ultimately to be an attempt to test the rules of an emerging reality principle rather than a symbolic articulation of his own unconscious phantasies. For Fritz, the fantasy of a forest serves as a kind of daunting horizon between civilisation and wildness, from a world of meaning and order to a world of chaos and disorder. Later in the same article, Klein draws from the work of Sándor Ferenczi to continue to explore the psychic potential of the forest fantasy as presented in the analysis of Fritz. Expanding Freud's Oedipal conflict into a broader, existential battle between the reality and pleasure principles, Klein argues the forest to be a 'curious' realm, curiosity being a key emotion to balance the desire for affirmation and stasis with the tendency towards expansion and knowledge that is at the heart of Freud's own battle between life and death within the human psyche (1921, p. 19).

In what follows, I hope to extend these brief numerations on the forest contained in Klein's own analysis into a Kleinian-inspired topology of forests within recent examples of fantasy cinema. Taking inspiration from her early objects of infancy, I argue that the forest's liminal status as something partially beyond human interaction and partially a consequence of human interaction makes it an extremely useful realm to use within fictions that interrogate the gap between the reality principle (a world defined by external laws) and the pleasure principle (a world of subjective order and stasis).

Fantasy fiction is fundamentally about the staging of the liminality between the world as it is and the world as it could be, gathering its energy from the hopes, aspirations and dreams out of 'the Desire and longing arising out of the promise of other worlds or states of being' (Wolfe, 1986, p. 136). Klein provides a useful framework to think through the persistence of fantasy forests within this storytelling world, arguing as she does that it is our capacity to imagine, rather than our capacity to be rational, that represent the perhaps most primordial aspect of the human experience. If this is true of our waking lives, it is true also of our fictions and the forests that spring up from our capacity to imagine.

(i): 'Bad' Forests

The dramatic and iconographic function of the 'bad' forest shares many similarities with Klein's concept of the 'bad' object (sometimes referred to as the 'bad' mother or breast). For Klein, the subject's early ability to create psychic objects (what she often refers to as 'imagos') relates to an early stage of infant development she refers to as 'paranoid–schizoid' (1975e, pp. 199–209; 1975f, p. 154; 1975d, pp. 1–24). The paranoid–schizoid stage of development represents the earliest encounters between the child and the external world wherein the scenarios he or she encounters is not understood logically as a part of coherent system of patterns and principles, but as series of emotional moments that are often highly anxious as the young subject struggles to comprehend that which they experience. These moments can be divided into 'good' and 'bad', with good moments representing encounters with scenarios that the subject finds pleasing and comforting, and bad moments representing that which he or she finds anxiety-making or persecutory in tone.

Both these 'good' and 'bad' tendencies serve crucial psychic functions. They do not merely reflect the child's experiences of the world; they are the first stage in a child making meaning out of that world, even if that meaning is by its very nature limited to an emotional rather than logical understanding. It is through encountering 'good' and 'bad' objects that the child learns there is a world, processing it by projecting bad parts of the self – feelings of anxiety and general displeasure – on to the world as a means of trying to control and destroy the external objects encountered (Segal, 2003, p. 37).

The bad object is therefore not altogether that bad. Instead, the bad object possesses an important function to allow unconscious phantasies to take shape, allowing the subject to begin to comprehend the frightening internal and external worlds he or she is struggling to understand. As the child develops and matures, the function of creative activities like play in childhood is to allow for the expression of subjective states of being that seem to be in conflict with the reality principle. Play has what Klein terms a 'libinidial cathexis', even the troubling kind (1975a, p. 78). Prior to the formation of conscious thought, anxiety is not repressed as it often is in later life. Instead, anxiety is expressed through phantasy. The very function of the bad object is to provide a locus for the anxious feelings to be channelled into, allowing the child to achieve a feeling of mastery of his or her emotions through their projection on to the world. As Klein argues, 'in games and phantasies he lives through as part of his instinctive impulses, especially of the Oedipus complex, uninhibited; if for instance he listens with pleasure to the Grimm's fairy-tales without subsequent anxiety-manifestations' (1975a, p. 52). The 'bad' object is, after all, not a real enemy or threat. As Klein argues, contrary to the increase of anxiety, the creation of a 'bad' object allows the subject to ward off the internal threat of the often-tyrannical super-ego (1975e, p. 201).

'Bad' forests perform a similar function within the context of fantasy cinema to the bad object. Certain features that separate the forest as distinct from cultivated space (wildness, harshness, unruliness) are emphasised within a narrative that seeks to utilise such qualities as part of its dramatic system, offering a threatening realm of drama and suspense that seems rooted in the same persecutory anxieties identified by Klein in her analysis of the child's early development. Perhaps a quintessential example of such a 'bad' forest comes in the initial introduction of Fangorn in *The Lord of the Rings: The Two Towers* (Peter Jackson, 2002). Within Tolkien's novel, Fangorn is simultaneously as a place full of history (Legolas the elf describes Fangorn as 'very old … and full of memory') and a place that denies comprehension (Pippin describes it as 'very dim, and stuffy'). In the cinematic adaptation, Fangorn is first depicted through a series of framing devices that emphasise this sense of the anxiety of not knowing as the narration crosscuts between its various storylines for dramatic effect.

The forest is introduced in the narrative as the place where Aragorn loses the ability to track the hobbits' footprints as they lead inside. Through a transitionary edit, contrasting from day to night and from open field to thick woodland, a scene shows the two hobbits Merry and Pippin then entering Fangorn to escape a hoard of chasing orcs. The framing places the two tiny figures of the hobbits in the centre of the frame as the camera pans backwards to reveal a tangle of trees, branches and foliage, making the space both full and empty at the same time. Fangorn is full of details but empty of coherent meaning. Fangorn is a mixture of an abundance of backstory and meaning, and yet an acknowledgement that one cannot access that meaning inside it.

The use of a 'bad' forest as a dramatic device or location allows a fantasy narrative like *The Lord of the Rings* to offer opportunities for its audiences to engage with such anxieties as part of the narrative trajectory. 'Bad' forests like Fangorn appear repeatedly through many of the most popular fantasy franchises of the last decades. In the *Harry Potter* film series, the dark forest functions again as a key place in which narrative tension is increased and often the storyline progressed through the revelation or allusion to secrets contained within the wood.

In *Harry Potter and the Philosopher's Stone* (Chris Columbus, 2001), the dark forest is introduced when Harry and his friends serve a detention with the Hogwart's groundskeeper Hagrid. Like Fangorn, the forest is set up as place with untold secrets and creatures, a description aided by the scene taking place at night with a low lighting style to highlight the presence of characters but to obscure the finer details of the setting. As they enter, like Fangorn, the filmmaking patterns shift from a personal to an impersonal register, shifting from a series of close-up shots designed to highlight the conflict between Harry and Draco as they are put to task in the forest to shots of their bodies framed against the backdrop of the forest itself. Branches are frequently placed in the foreground of shots, whilst the contrasting lighting places elements of each frame in deep shadow, all of which contribute to a sense of not knowing that is further emphasised by the revelation of a hooded figure (later revealed to be Voldemort) drinking unicorn blood.

Similar scenes appear throughout the series, whether this be the spider attack in *Harry Potter and the Chamber of Secrets* (Chris Columbus, 2002) as Harry and Ron drive their stolen car through the dark wood, the confrontation between Dolores Umbridge and the centaurs in *Harry Potter and the the Order of the Phoenix* (David Yates, 2007), or else Harry's Christ-like act of sacrifice (before his eventual rebirth) to Voldemort in *Harry Potter and the Deathly Hallows: Part Two* (David Yates, 2011). The forest is continually represented as both revelatory and mysterious, its fear caused by a feeling that characters interrupt a great chain of creatures and plants working together as part of a mysterious, frightening ecosystem.

A more violent, hyper-realist version of the 'bad' forest also takes place in *The Hunger Games* (Gary Ross, 2012), wherein the entire gaming zone plays out in a large dense forest. As established in the film's atmospheric opening scenes, Katniss finds solace in the forest due its ability to be away from society. This same feature becomes a source of the threat and otherness of the gaming zone, offset against the watching hyper-stylised residents of the urban capital. This is a key aspect of the disorientation achieved in the film's Cornucopia sequence, as the film's visual palette shifts from the steel grey tubes of the capital's machines to the leafy foliage of the forest, a source of both fear and safety as the murderous contest starts.

The use of a 'bad' forest as a dramatic device or location, then, allows a fantasy narrative to offer opportunities for its audiences to engage with such anxieties over the basic threat external objects pose our psychic equilibrium. They dramatise the fact the world has the capacity to be unknown, to be threatening and to force the self to release that they are a tiny aspect of a world, rather than the world itself. A good case study of how this dramatic function of the 'bad' forest functions to both emphasise and complicate some of the psychic undertones of the kind of folkloric imagery analysed by psychoanalytic theorists like Bettelheim is provided in the revisionist retelling of the Grimm story of Snow White, *Snow White and the Huntsman* (Rupert Sanders, 2012). Partially readapted to reflect more progressive gender attitudes and partially in order to adhere to many of the conventions of the contemporary fantasy franchise, *Snow White and the Huntsman* makes heavy use of the forest scene within its narrative as a site of conflict, mystery and what Frances Pheasant-Kelly terms as 'abject spectacle' (65).

The film's opening battle sequence stages the forest as a site of conflict, making use of harsh, visceral edits and a soundscape that emphasises force and strength through the impact of battle. After this initial conflict, the forest is then positioned somewhat differently as place of mystery. It is the place from which the evil queen Ravenna emerges, the forest's secrecy masking the source of threat she contains. This pairing of Ravenna with the forest is emphasised through the film, her corruption of the kingdom occurring in parallel with the destruction of the forest's fertility as plants rot and petrify. The forest also serves a key character function. The figure of the Huntsman, elevated to the status of titular character, becomes key to Snow White's blossoming into a warrior queen through his mastery of the forest environment. The film's resolution of female empowerment is forged through the partnership of a youth and masculine guidance, all of which revolves around the relationship between Snow White, Ravenna and the Huntsman to the forest environment that is often hostile and difficult to comprehend.

This triangular relationship between the three main characters of *Snow White and the Huntsman* contains many of the same quasi-Oedipal dynamics analysed by Bettelheim and others within the original folk tale, giving the forest a function as a symbol of both paternal authority and female sexuality. Yet, such an interpretation does an injustice to its mystery of the forest – the function it serves as a source of drama and tension. Instead, in the hands of Hollywood's production, the forest becomes a far more malleable place whereby audiences can bring a number of associations and connotations under the guise of 'bad' object relations. As the Huntsman says to Snow White, the 'Forest gains its strength from your weakness'. The 'bad' forest is thus not a symbol, but a psychic space that resonates with primordial anxieties of being alive in a world.

(ii): 'Good' Forests

In Kleinian theory, the formation of the imago of the 'good' object within early infant relations is a consequence of both the biological and societal role of the mother. For Klein, early object relations are formulated through a

combination of projective and introjective phantasies. The child must simultaneously place on to the world his or her own emotional state and
produce an emotional state by taking in qualities of the world. By way of an
example, the bad breast is formed by the child taking in (introjecting)
qualities that are external to a particular sensory moment, i.e. the breast's
inability to provide nourishment in a particular moment. This perceived
lack in the world becomes a lack in the self, triggering anxiety and persecutory fears, which in turn are projected back on to the breast to make it
responsible for those fears. The object becomes 'bad' because it makes the
child feel bad. The good breast functions similarly. The child takes in the
perceived positive qualities of the nourishing, pleasurable breast as a way of
building his or her own sense of ego, or identity, allowing emotional and
intellectual growth to occur within an emotional backdrop of security
provided. For Klein, the good is therefore synonymous from an early age
with the maternal, the subject structured to negotiate his or her own sense
of identity by craving the security of the imagined good breast (1975b, p.
179).

The typical usages of the 'good' forest as a setting within contemporary
fantasy cinema have strong connotations with the same maternal qualities
Klein identifies in early child object relations. In *Snow White and the
Huntsman*, for example, the dark mysterious forest discussed previous is
contrasted with a vision of a forest that embodies fertility and safety. In the
sequence in which Snow White visits the home of the dwarfs, the idyllic
woodland realm they inhabited is referred to as 'sanctuary'. This idyllic
home is buried within the dark woods and contrasts with the barren and
mysterious qualities of the aforementioned dark forest through its abundance of colourful foliage, open green expanses and a cluster of wildlife that
lives in harmony with the dwarfs. The spectacle displayed in this sequence
is utopic in both the general usage of the term and in relation to Richard
Dyer's specific qualities of entertainment, offering a woodland realm that
represents transparency as opposed to secrecy, community as opposed to
isolationism, and energy as opposed to reservation (1992, p. 26).

Similar scenes occur in a number of other fantasy films produced over the
past two decades, often functioning either as a pause in the narrative stakes,
allowing the characters (and by proxy the audience) a respite from the
tension of the drama, or else a place for forgotten values to be restored.
Christopher Robin (Marc Forster, 2018), Disney's latest sequel/reboot of the
Winnie-the-Pooh franchise, constructs a narrative in which the iconic hundred-acre wood functions as a key site of familial restoration, infantilisation
and nourishment. In the original novels, this 'good' forest served as a safe
space to allow the animal creatures to come to life without the rules or logics
of reality invading upon the stories. In *Christopher Robin*, it functions as place
where the now-adult Christopher Robin must return to the sanctuary of the
woodland space, away from his family and the societal pressures of his job

that have transformed him from a fun-loving child to a stern adult in order to be restored as *the* Christopher Robin of the original A.A. Milne tales. The film uses the site of the 'good' forest as part of its nostalgic attempt to re-energise the central stories and characters of the Winnie-the-Pooh tales for a new generation.

These examples of nurturing, maternal 'good' forests function within their respective narratives to instil a feeling of calm in the protagonists within a scenario that is otherwise fraught with anxiety. This is in keeping with both the psychic dynamics of early object relations and indeed with the repercussions of such dynamics within the wider structuring of the psyche in later life. Once established in the ego, the internalised good object is expressed not simply through the subject's desire for a particular external object or person, such as the mother's breast. Rather, it is the ideal of the good object that structures desire itself, creating the potential for further anxiety when that desire is denied. As Klein argues, 'pleasurable situations, actually experienced or phantasied, remained indeed unconscious and fixated' (1975a, p. 87). Play allows for the subject to discharge this tension, this desire for the good object, making conscious the subject's longing and enacting it out to achieve sublimation.

The phantasies surrounding good objects are therefore not simply a desire for the qualities of the good breast but a replacement of the bad with the good. This is why so many idyllic fantasy forests are placed within a narrative of deforestation. The spectacular jungles of *Avatar* (James Cameron, 2009), a key selling point of the film's 3D graphics, enact similar Kleinian dynamics of nourishment, safety and security, the relationship between the Na'avi and the environment seemingly overtly maternal. Yet, the spectacle of the forests of Pandora is emphasised throughout a narrative that threatens their destruction, emphasising the 'good' qualities of Pandora against the possibility of their removal or destruction.

Whilst the maternal features of the good forest are consistent across a range of different fantasy films, the function of the Kleinian-inspired topology I propose is not to focus on the potential unconscious symbolism embedded within its representation. The 'good' forest does not just represent maternal qualities. It uses these maternal qualities as a platform for characters and audiences alike to engage in imaginative activities outside the sphere of meaning-making that constitutes everyday life. Pandora is not just a symbolic realm but an imaginative realm; the hundred-acre wood is not just nostalgic for the past but for a fantasy world once shared amongst popular culture that has now lost some of its vibrancy and ubiquity. The invitation provided by the 'good' forest to play within its walls without fear of judgement or oppression is key to its psychic function, allowing for the discharge of anxiety through the working-through or negative emotions and respite from the 'bad' objects and persecutory fears they embody. The imagined 'good' object of the mother allows for a feeling of security to emerge within the subject that is crucial for all future positive emotional relationships, encouraging the child to trust in his or her environment enough to explore it through a process of imaginative thinking (1975c, p. 307).

A good example of this key function of the 'good' forest is provided in the children's fantasy film *Bridge to Terabithia* (Gábor Csupó, 2007). Telling the story of the friendship between young adolescents Jesse and Leslie, the eponymous magical woodland is not a 'real' fictional world comparable with that of Narnia or Middle-earth (real in the context of the narrative). Rather, Terabithia is a self-consciously imagined land created by Jesse and Leslie as a way of both playing together and acting out their social anxieties. In Terabithia, school bullies are transformed into troublesome creatures from whom they must survive attacks, or else giants they must subdue and pacify, the two using the veneer of fantasy to express and conquer the trauma of their suffering. The purpose of Terabithia is not to return Jesse and Leslie to an infantile state reliant on the presence of the maternal forest. Instead, the presence of the 'good' forest provides the security to enact conflict and drama, the wood offering a suitable distance from reality for them to use it as a psychic battleground much like the spectacular set-pieces in which the two leads go to battle against the various fantasy creatures they imagine. Jesse and Leslie are able to perform this act of play by being in Terabithia, a place within the woods that can only be accessed through a rope bridge they construct. The 'good' forest behind their respective homes provides distance and perspective on the society they leave behind.

When the narrative takes a tragic turn as Leslie dies whilst playing in the woods alone, the bridge that once protected Leslie and Jesse from the society they wished to temporarily escape becomes tainted by its associations with death. However, far from vilifying the space in which Leslie's death occurs, the narrative goes on to celebrate Terabithia as a place that provides the safety and security for Jesse to console his grief in fantasy. After hearing the news of her drowning, Jesse retreats into the woodland space to enact fantasies of his lost friend, hearing her voice, returning to the spaces in which they used to play and reacting angrily when his little sister tries to join him there, preferring the isolation provided by the wood. When his father tries to console his son with the reality of the situation, Jesse envisions him as a faceless monster, running from him further and further into the forest. Neither able to live within the forest forever given that this would require a level of existence outside the realm of society nor able to give up his need for Terabithia, the film climaxes with Jesse building a permanent bridge to the 'good' forest that he can access safely at any time. To step into the 'good' forest is to step into a nurturing realm of fantasy.

Conclusion

There are many different types of forests, many different types of fantasy films and many different types of people. The relationship between psychoanalysis and fantasy fiction has been historically fruitful but not always productive. At its best, psychoanalysis provides a critical vocabulary to explore the psychic resonances of images and scenarios that seem so divorced from everyday life. At its most unpersuasive, psychoanalysis offers strict dogma and overbearing structures, transforming the multiplicity of the human experience into a series of tick boxes and check lists. I have no wish to do this to the fantasy forest.

Whilst being initially profitable in lending scholarly legitimacy to the academic study of the fairy tale, Freudian psychoanalysis has also been criticised for providing an overly rigid decoding of the various elements that make up the fairy tale, an approach epitomised in Bettelheim's *The Uses of Enchantment*. The Kleinian topology I propose is not intended to subscribe fixed definitions or interpretations, nor is it offered as an attempt to rigidly slice the recent examples of popular fantasy cinema into two. Instead, I wish to offer the start of a psychic taxonomy that offers tentative explanations as to why the forest functions as such a useful device within contemporary fantasy media. Whilst Freudian theory views phantasies of the forest, and phantasy in general, as a psychic device that expresses the repressed unconscious mechanisms of the human mind, Kleinian theories of phantasy instead consider it as a form of meaning-making that operates in closer dialogue with more rational processes developed after the subject's adaptation to the reality principle. The fantasy forest therefore provides a means of psychic expression that stresses the emotional and pre-logical attachments the subject has with the world, attachments that operate both in tandem with and in opposition to his or her attempts to understand the world of reality.

References

Bettelheim, B. (1976), *The Uses of Enchantment: The Meaning and Importance of Fairy Tales*. London: Thames & Hudson.

Bordwell, D. (1996), 'Contemporary Film Studies and the Vicissitudes of Grand Theory' in D. Bordwell & N. Carroll (eds), *Post-Theory: Reconstructing Film Studies*, Madison: Wisconsin University Press, pp. 3–36.

Creed, C. (1993), *The Monstrous-Feminine: Film, Feminism, Psychoanalysis*, London & New York: Routledge.

Dunn, A. (1988), 'The Indian Boy's Dream Wherein Every Mother's Son Rehearses His Part: Shakespeare's *A Midsummer Night's Dream*', *Shakespeare Studies*, Vol. 20, pp. 15–32.

Dyer, R. (1992), 'Entertainment and Utopia' in *Only Entertainment*, London & New York: Routledge, pp. 19–35.

Elms, A.C. (2001), 'Apocryphal Freud: Sigmund Freud's Most Famous "Quotations" and their Actual Sources', *Annual of Psychoanalysis*, Vol. 29, pp. 83–104.

Freud, S. (1964), 'New Introductory Lectures on Psycho-analysis (1933)' in *The Standard Edition of the Complete Psychological Works of Sigmund Freud: Volume XXII*, London: The Hogarth Press, pp. 1–182.

Furby, J. & Hines, C. (2012), *Fantasy*, London & New York: Routledge.

Gillison, G. (1994), 'Symbolic Homosexuality and Cultural Theory: The Unconscious Meaning of Sister Exchange Among the Gimi of Highland New Guinea' in S. Heald & A. Deluz (eds), *Anthropology and Psychoanalysis: An Encounter Through Culture*, London: Routledge, pp. 210–224.

Harris, J.M. (2008), *Folklore and the Fantastic in Nineteenth-Century British Fiction*, Aldershot & Burlington: Ashgate.

Klein, M. (1975a), 'Early Analysis (1923)' in *Love, Guilt and Reparation and Other Works 1921–1945*, London: The Hogarth Press, pp. 77–105.

Klein, M. (1975b), 'Envy and Gratitude (1957)' in *Envy and Gratitude and Other Works 1946–1963*, London: The Hogarth Press, pp. 176–235.

Klein, M. (1975c), 'Love, Guilt and Reparation (1937)' in *Love, Guilt and Reparation and Other Works 1921–1945*, London: The Hogarth Press, pp. 306–343.

Klein, M. (1975d), 'Notes on Some Schizoid Mechanisms (1946)' in *Envy and Gratitude and Other Works 1946–1963*, London: The Hogarth Press, pp. 1–24.

Klein, M. (1975e), 'Personification in the Play of Children (1929)' in *Love, Guilt and Reparation and Other Works 1921–1945*, London: The Hogarth Press, pp. 199–209.

Klein, M. (1975f), *The Psycho-Analysis of Children* [1932], London: The Hogarth Press.

McGowan, T. (2003), 'Looking for the Gaze: Lacanian Film Theory and Its Vicissitudes', *Cinema Journal*, Vol. 42, No. 3, pp. 27–47.

Pheasant-Kelly, F. (2013), *Fantasy Film Post 9/11*, New York: Palgrave MacMillan.

Segal, J. (2003), *Melanie Klein*, London: SAGE.

Sobchack, V. (1992), *The Address of the Eye: A Phenomenology of Film Experience*, Princeton: Princeton University Press.

Solomon, I. (1995), *A Primer of Kleinian Therapy*, Northvale: Jason Aronson.

Tyrer, B. (2016), *Out of the Past: Lacan and Film Noir*, London: Palgrave.

Walters, J. (2011), *Fantasy Film: A Critical Introduction*, Oxford & New York: Berg.

Wolfe, G.K. (1986), *Critical Terms of Science Fiction and Fantasy: A Glossary and Guide to Scholarship*, Westport: Greenwood Press.

Zipes, J. (2011), *The Enchanted Screen: The Unknown History of Fairy-Tale Films*, New York & Abingdon: Routledge.

Part 3

Tolkien's Forests

Chapter 7

Trees and Tolkien: Reflections Between Medieval and Modern Reverence

Brad Eden

A number of recent studies on the Anglo-Saxon attitude towards trees in early Germanic and Christian worship have been published in the past six years, all of them focusing on different aspects and uses of trees in the daily life, worship, and understanding of ancient and medieval British and Anglo-Saxon society. These books include Cusack (2011), Hooke (2013), Bintley and Shapland (2013), and Bintley (2015).

This intense interest in trees and their practical and sacred uses in both medieval pagan and Christian contexts in Britain in the past six years corresponds with the posthumous publication of a number of works of J.R.R. Tolkien (1892–1973), whose well-known love for trees and the natural world is found in *The Lord of the Rings* (1954–1955) as well as various other writings and stories related to his mythology. These posthumous publications include *The Legend of Sigurd & Gudrun* (2009; written in the early 1930s), *The Fall of Arthur* (2013; written in the early 1930s), *The Story of Kullervo* (2014; written sometime from 1912–1916) and *The Lay of* Aotrou *and* Itroun (2017; written in 1930). These, what I would call 'new' Tolkien publications, provide an interesting perspective on his development and the use of trees, woods, and forests in his writings, many of which were written prior to the genesis of *The Lord of the Rings*.

I want to focus attention on the reverence towards trees, sacred groves, and wooden pillars by medieval Germanic societies, and the leverage used by Anglo-Saxon missionaries in both England and on the continent to see the 'rood' or cross of Christ as a replacement for pagan worship of trees as they attempted to convert these peoples from the seventh through the tenth centuries. Given Tolkien's background in Old English and Anglo-Saxon studies, his use of the liminal power and boundaries inherent in trees and forests combines both a reverence and respect that has much in common with current scholarship on this topic.

Reverence for trees in the ancient and medieval world

Both the Greeks and the Romans link a reverence for trees with their gods. The oak tree was associated with Zeus/Jupiter and the sacred grove of Dodona is often mentioned in ancient sources as a sacred oak grove dedicated to Zeus. The ancient Germanic peoples did not simply live in forests; they worshipped in them and they revered the trees they contained. Trees were at the very heart of their religious life. Many Roman historians mention early encounters with Germanic peoples and their religious practices involving trees and sacred groves of trees, which I won't recount here.

Anglo-Saxon society inherited the love and worship of trees, as is often mentioned in both conversion and Old English literature. As examples, pagan shrines were often sited near sacred trees and wells, and the strategy of St Augustine of Canterbury and St Gregory the Great in their conversion efforts in the seventh century indicate that these pagan shrines were often left standing in order to support a smooth transition to Christianity, while the trees were cut down and used to help build new churches. In fact, the Old English word for 'cross' is not based on the Latin word *crux* but on Anglo-Saxon words related to trees such as *rood*, treow and *beam*. In Bintley and Shapland (2013), there is an entire chapter on the importance of early conversion and missionary efforts of linking sacred trees and their imagery to the cross of Christ, showing how place names and Anglo-Saxon cult sites indicate this focus. An example is the northern royal fort at Yeavering and the archaeological evidence of its large tree beam as a central worship point.

The movement from sacred pagan shrine to a Christian church was often associated with the missionary cutting down sacred trees in the vicinity and building a new church from the wood, a kind of transference of power from one religion to another. This power transference is highlighted in the Old English poem *The Dream of the Rood*, where the tree upon which Christ is crucified actually talks to the reader about its experience of moving from living tree to an instrument of death to a symbol of life and hope, all captured and caught up in the drama of anthropomorphism and symbolism.

Two real-life examples of how early missionaries cut down sacred trees in order to convert people are documented by St Boniface and Charlemagne in the eighth century. According to his early biographer, Boniface started to chop the Donar oak down (better known as the Jupiter oak) near the present-day town of Fritzlar in northern Hesse, when suddenly a great wind, as if by miracle, blew the ancient oak over. When the god did not strike him down, the people were amazed and converted to Christianity. He built a chapel dedicated to Saint Peter from its wood at the site and the chapel was the beginning of the monastery in Fritzlar. In 772 at the temple of Tanfana near Paderborn, Charlemagne and his troops cut down the Irminsul, a tree sacred to the Saxon god Irmin, which the Saxons believed supported the universe.

Bede illustrates the importance of the tree/cross imagery when he describes the Christian king Oswald of Northumbria's raising of the cross before his famous battle at Hefenfeld (often called Heavenfield), which he won over the native Britons of the region. That wooden cross became a holy relic after Oswald's defeat under the pagan king Penda of Mercia and its pieces (as well as the pieces of Oswald's body) enjoyed an international reputation both in England and especially on the Continent.

Trees also acted as boundary markers between parishes, districts, and even peoples in the early Middle Ages, which is expressly detailed in the various books mentioned earlier. A particular example is Augustine's Oak mentioned in Bede, which was used as a meeting place between the British and Roman priests on the border of the Hwicce in the early seventh century. The fact that early Anglo-Saxon homes and churches were built of wood instead of stone (except for specific examples) indicates the preference and comfort of this particular material for building; in fact, the Anglo-Saxons developed a number of techniques for 'farming trees' as building material.

These techniques included coppicing (where trees do not die when they are cut down, but sprout from buds around the base of the trunk to produce large numbers of narrow poles). Since the tree already has a developed root system, pole growth is very rapid, and they can be harvested every 10 years. Another technique is pollarding: cutting the trunk and lower branches a meter or two off the ground. This technique promotes the growth of numerous shoots, and is better than coppicing because the shoots are sited well away from browsing animals and flood waters. In early Welsh literature, from the Book of Taliesin whose history may go back to the sixth century, there is the poem called 'Cad Goddau', or 'The Battle of the Trees', which contains a tree-list of 34 named trees, shrubs, and flowers, the fullest medieval Welsh tree-list extant. Tree-lists are common in many early societies, but in this particular poem, these leafy creatures similar to the Ents in Tolkien's Middle-earth have a mock-heroic battle, a unique story that has survived from the Celtic Heroic Age.

The Vikings and Norse religions also indicate a veneration for trees, forests, and woods. Whenever a tree appears in a skaldic stanza, its audience knows at once to expect not a leafy source of nuts or firewood, but a person. The sayings 'tree equals man' and 'When we chop down a tree, however necessary the action is, we are aware that we are losing one of our own' are two of the most commonplace in the Old Norse poetic tradition. In the Norse Voluspa, the creation of humankind is from two pieces of driftwood, one of ash and the other of elm, named Askr and Embla. The world tree Yggdrasil supports the nine worlds of the cosmos.

Early Irish and Celtic traditions show great respect towards sacred trees and groves. Sacred trees and groves were liminal spaces, often only accessed by druids, priests, or even early Irish Christian saints. The five sacred trees of Ireland, each linked to their own provinces, hostels, and roads, are part of a pre-Christian cosmology rooted in a five-fold division of space. These trees were called the Ancient Tree of Tortu (Bile Tortan), the Yew of Ross (Eo Ruis), the Yew of Mugna (Eo Mugna), Dathi's Branch (Craeb Daithi), and the ancient tree of Uisnech (Bile Uisneg). Of these five trees, three of them are ashes (Tortu, Daithi, Uisneg) and two are yews (Ross, Mugna).

The importance of hazel-nuts both as givers of wisdom as well as fodder for pig grazing appears in numerous Irish legends and early Christian stories. Because Ireland was never conquered by Rome, its contact with early Christianity brought about a unique blend of pagan and secular oral and written literature in which trees, druids and saints are in constant interplay and interaction. Trees associated with sacred wells, with royal consecration sites, with ecclesiastical foundations and with saints are abundant.

For instance, one cosmogonic myth connects the five sacred trees of Ireland with two specific mythological characters recorded in the Middle Irish tale 'The Settling of the Possessions of Tara'. One of these characters is Fintan mac Bochra, known as the oldest man in Ireland, since he is a survivor of the antediluvian flood of Noah that brought about the destruction of the world in the Bible. Fintan is often associated with Amorgen the chief fili or poet who leads the Milesians against the Tuatha de Danann. Fintan is one of the links between Ireland's pagan past and its Christian beginnings. The other mythological character associated with trees is the giant Trefhuilngid, who often appears with a huge tree branch in his right hand, which supposedly comes from Paradise and carries the seeds of the five sacred trees.

Another influence on early Irish literature is the Gnostic tenth-century Irish apocryphon *The Ever-New Tongue*, which features the Apostle Philip and a number of Hebrew wise men gathered on Mount Zion on Easter eve. Philip's proclamations and wisdom regarding the future so incense the gathered wise men that they order to have his tongue cut out. However, after doing this four or five times, and with Philip continuing to answer questions and dispense information despite the fact that his tongue continues to be cut out, it is obvious to those gathered that he is a messenger from God. One of the mysteries that Philip reveals to the wise men is the story of the trees planted by God at the creation of the world. Philip says 'It is reasonable that you should ask that, for there are four of those trees in which it is thought that there are soul and intelligence like the life of angels.' Philip then goes on to relate the wonders of these four primeval trees, along with the central tree of life from Paradise. Whether this story, based on the Greek Acts of Philip from the fourth to fifth centuries, may be the basis of the five primeval trees of Ireland, will never be known, but qualities of the trees are very similar in both the pagan and the Irish Christian tradition.

There are also a few stories about the fall of these five primeval trees in Ireland during the first Age of the Saints, generally the fifth to sixth centuries. For instance, in the Old Irish text on St Molling's birth and life, the fall of one of these trees is described through prayer and fasting, and the wood is used to build a wooden oratory in the monastery, similar to the tales around the Anglo-Saxon missions such as St Augustine of Canterbury and St Boniface in Germany. The Old Irish tree-list also has four classes of importance into which the twenty-eight principal trees and shrubs are divided which were known in early medieval Ireland. The seven most important trees are oak, hazel, holly, yew, ash, Scots pine and the wild apple tree. The Class B trees are alder, willow, hawthorn, rowan, birch, elm and wild cherry. Class C trees include blackthorn, elder, spindle-tree, whitebeam, arbutus, aspen and juniper. Finally, the Class D group (a mix of trees and shrubs) includes bracken, bog-myrtle, gorse, bramble, heather, broom and wild rose.

In the Indic religions, the five trees of Paradise are named, and they play a significant cosmological role in the Puranas, which are ancient Hindu texts that eulogise various deities. The trees are named and are also linked to five earthly trees. The later syncretic Manichaean tradition, which is a mixture of Gnostic and Christian Zoroastrianism, contains a dualistic image of two different types of primeval trees: five trees of darkness, which embody the material world; and five trees of light, which descend from the spiritual world. For instance, the fourth-century Coptic text, *The* Kephalaia *of the Teacher*, describes how the five trees of darkness were cultivated by matter from the five elements (namely, smoke, fire, wind, water and darkness) and that all matter was embodied in these trees. The Manichaean tradition is the only one where cosmological trees are associated with light and darkness.

Tolkien and trees

There have already been quite a few studies on Tolkien's references to trees, forests and woods in relation to his Anglo-Saxon and Old English roots. One of the most recognized forests from ancient and medieval sources is Myrkviðr or Mirkwood. As Tolkien comments in a letter to his grandson:

> Mirkwood is not an invention of mine, but a very ancient name, weighted with legendary associations. It was probably the Primitive Germanic name for the great mountainous forest regions that anciently formed a barrier to the south of the lands of Germanic expansion. In some traditions it became used especially of the boundary between Goths and Huns. I speak now from memory: its ancientness seems indicated by its appearance in very early German (11th c.?) as mirkiwidu although the *merkw- stem 'dark' is not otherwise found in German at all (only in O[ld] E[nglish], O[ld] S[axon], and O[ld] N[orse]), and the stem *widu- > witu was in German (I think) limited to the sense of 'timber,' not very common, and did not survive into mod[ern] G[erman]. In O[ld] E[nglish] mirce only survives in poetry, and in the sense 'dark', or rather 'gloomy', only in Beowulf [line] 1405 ofer myrcan mor: elsewhere only with the sense 'murky' wicked, hellish. It was never, I think, a mere 'colour' word: 'black', and was from the beginning weighted with the sense of 'gloom'... (Tolkien, 1981: 369–370).

The name Mirkwood is found in the poems in the Old Norse Poetic Edda, and refers to a mythical forest. In other eddic poems it separates the human world from the supernatural world of the gods and/or divides the land of the Goths from the land of the Huns. Philologically, Dr Tom Shippey indicates that Mirkwood's use by Grimm, Tolkien and William Morris sees the forest as a mythic association or cultural memory lost in linguistic and imaginary time as a 'boundary' or 'border' association with dark meanings.

The localisation of Myrkviðr varies by source:

- The Maeotian marshes, which separated the Goths from the Huns in the Norse Hervarar *saga*

- The forest that separates the Huns from the Burgundians

- Kolmarden ('the dark forest'), in Sweden, in Sogubrot and in legends such as that of *Helge* Hundingsbane

- The forest south of Uppsala in Styrbjarnar thattr Sviakappa (the present remnant of this forest is called Lunsen)

- Uncertain locations, such as in the Volundarkvitha, where it is probably located somewhere else in Scandinavia

- Besides the various references to the power of trees and forests in *The Lord of the Rings*, including The Old Forest, Fangorn, and and Lorien, Tolkien mentions Mirkwood specifically in many of the 'new' publications mentioned earlier. I am going to discuss each of these separately.

Legend of Sigurd & Gudrun (2009)

There are four mentions of Mirkwood in this tale, which Tolkien wrote in the 1930s but wasn't published until 2009:

1. Lay of the Volsungs, VII, p. 131

> By mighty Mirkwood
> On the marches of the East
> The great Goth-kings
> In glory ruled.
> By Danpar-banks
> Was dread warfare
> With the hosts of Hunland,
> Horsemen countless

2. Lay of Gudrun, stanza 6, p. 255

> From mighty Mirkwood
> Came message darkly
> 'Atli ariseth
> Armies mustering.
> Hate awakens,

Hosts are arming;
Under horses' hooves
Hunland trembles!'

3. Lay of Gudrun, stanza 83, p. 280

Atli sat there
Anger burned him;
Yet murmurs mounted,
Men were rising.
Goths were there many:
Griefs remembered,
Wars in Mirkwood
And wars of old.

4. Appendix C, Fragments of a heroic poem of Attila in Old English, p. 369, 371 (based on Old Norse Atlakvitha), stanza 20–24

He said that he would give you Gnitanheath,
Give into your power the wide woodland,
Shrieking spear and golden prow,
Great treasures, the abodes of the Dnieper,
And that forest renowned that is called Mirkwood.

Christopher Tolkien discusses his father's use of Mirkwood in his notes to these tales:

> Not occurring in the Saga, the Norse name Myrkvithr, Anglicized as 'Mirkwood', was used of a dark boundary-forest, separating peoples, and is found in poems of the Edda in different applications; but it seems probable that in its origin it represented a memory in heroic legend of the great forest that divided the land of the Goths from the land of the Huns far off in the south and east. This is what the name means in the Eddaic poem Atlakvitha, the lay of Atli (Attila), whence its appearance in the Lay (Tolkien, 2009, p. 227).

> We may notice also the old traditional *vin* Borgunda of Gunnar, and the Myrkvithr (Mirkwood) specially associated with ancient Hun-stories" (Tolkien, 2009, p. 313).

The Fall of Arthur (2013)

There are two mentions of Mirkwood in this tale that was written in the early 1930's.

1. I, stanza 68, p. 19
(Arthur and knights traveling eastward, conquering heathen kings)

Foes before them, flames behind them
Ever east and onwardeager rode they,

And folk fled themas the face of God
Till earth was empty,and no eyes saw them,
And no ears heard themin the endless hills,
Save bird and beastbaleful haunting
The lonely lands.Thus at last came they
To Mirkwood's marginunder mountain-shadows;
Waste was behind them,walls before them;

2. I, stanza 132, p. 22

> Cold touched the heartsof the host encamped
> On Mirkwood's marginat the mountain-roots.
> They felt the forestthough the fogs veiled it;
> Their fires fainted.Fear clutched their souls,
> Waiting watchfulin a world of shadow
> For woe they knew not,no word speaking

Christopher Tolkien comments on Mirkwood in this book as well

> ...but a larger horizon seems to me to be suggested by the references to Mirkwood (I.68, 132). I cannot say whether my father intended a more precise meaning in his use of this ancient legendary name for a dark boundary forest separating peoples, but since Arthur's host marched 'from the mouths east and onwards' (I.62), and since the forest of Mirkwood lay 'on the houseless hills ever higher mounting/vast, unvanquished' (I.70-1) it seems that they were now far to the east of the regions of Saxon settlement; and this is strongly borne out by Sir Cradoc's word (I.153-4): 'While war ye wage on the wild peoples/in the homeless East...' (Tolkien, 2013, p. 86).

In *The Story of Kullervo*, one of Tolkien's earliest stories written between 1912 and 1916 but only recently published in 2014, there are no specific references to Mirkwood but the instructions from the Blue-Robed Lady of the Forest to Kullervo are quite implicit that he must avoid the wooded mountain on his return to his home, which she calls 'an evil wood' and indeed Kullervo's spite and avoidance of following the Blue-Robed Lady's advice directly leads to his downfall in the story.

In the *Lay of Aotrou & Itroun*, written by Tolkien in 1930 but not published until 2017, which is set in the Forest of Broceliande in Brittany, the editor makes these comments:

> Forest of Broceliande in medieval Brittany; 'the forest was a standard topos in medieval romance as a landscape contiguous with yet separate from reality, an "other" world which could on occasion become the actual Otherworld of Celtic myth. Combining real and symbolic associations, the forest became a literary construction with its own rules and associations. Tolkien's forests – Mirkwood, Nan Elmoth, Doriath, the Old Forest, Lorien, Fangorn – are some of the most recent in a long and distinguished line of descent.' Broceliand was used in Tolkien's *Lay of Leithian*, which he was in the middle of composing

when he wrote this Lay, and the name was changed to Beleriand by September of 1931 (Tolkien, 2017, p. 61).

In conclusion, this paper provides a quick overview of the importance of trees, forests, and woods in both ancient and medieval societies, and in the 'new' works of J.R.R. Tolkien, illustrating the unique connections and strands that mark both the medieval and modern reverence as well.

References

Bintley, M. & Shapland, M. (eds) (2013), *Trees and Timber in the Anglo-Saxon World*, Oxford: Oxford University Press.

Bintley, M. (2015), *Trees in the Religions of Early Medieval England*, Woodbridge, Suffolk: Boydell Press.

Cusack, C. (2011), *The Sacred Tree: Ancient and Medieval Manifestations*, Cambridge: Cambridge Scholars Publishing.

Hooke, D. (2013), *Trees in Anglo-Saxon England: Literature, Lore and Landscape*. Woodbridge, Suffolk: Boydell and Brewer Press.

Tolkien, J.R.R. (2013), *The Fall of Arthur*, Boston: HarperCollins.

_____. (2017), *The Lay of* Aotrou *and* Itroun, Boston: HarperCollins.

_____. (2009), *The Legend of Sigurd & Gudrun*, Boston: HarperCollins.

_____. (1981), *The letters of J.R.R. Tolkien*, Boston: Houghton Mifflin.

_____. (2014), *The Story of Kullervo*, Boston: HarperCollins.

Chapter 8

Shadow Shrouds and Moonlight Veils: The Forest as an Existential Scene in Tolkien's Legendarium

Leticia Cortina Aracil

In J.R.R. Tolkien's legendarium, landscapes are more than narrative settings; they are active agents of the action that takes place within them. Only rarely does this process happen in a clear, evident way through direct participation; instead, these sceneries typically provide a framework of meaning for the action they enable. This meaning takes significance through its coherence with the whole of Tolkien's sub-created universe, as a particular form or aspect of it. Furthermore, the elements of the landscape embody the usually veiled contribution of the divine powers to the development of the story. Forests are deeply meaningful agents in these accounts.

The woodlands written by Tolkien adhere to the mythologeme of the labyrinth (Kérenyi, 2006, pp. 51–52; Ronnberg & Martin, 2011, pp. 714–715). They are an *inner space* that, rather than closed or limited, is endowed with the amplitude inherent to all things liminal. Liminality involves the dissolution of an order, enabling something new to become established, and entering a forest poses an irresistible bifurcation in the possibilities of the adventurer's life. It means a prospect of encountering, between its shadows and nooks, realities that are not in proportion to the categories of their present existence, of how the world is understood by men, elves and even the Ainur. These encounters result in a vital stir that makes it impossible for the wanderer to return to their former way of living. This change, unlike any other that may be overcome in different sceneries of the legendarium, is intimately linked to the sphere of death in Arda (the world); in addition, the forest is the realm of power expressed through the wildness, the shadows, the moon, enchantment, and sleep.

This chapter will examine the narrative action of the forests in Tolkien's legendarium as the specific place for the *encounter* with the disproportion in this universe, with realities that break the categories by which the characters rule their existence: the marvellous and the monstrous. The approach to this will be an ontological reflection on the metaphysical rules that Tolkien developed for this cosmology. This structure gives consistency to Tolkien's diverse stories as a coherent whole, exploring even aspects of the legendarium that the author never explicitly explained.

First, a selection of exemplary cases from *The Silmarillion* (1977), *The Hobbit* (1937), and *The Lord of the Rings* (1954–1955) will be analysed by taking into account the vocabulary used to characterise the forests, the common structure that underlies the stories that take place within them and the experience of their protagonists. With this foundation provided, the particular conditions of liminality of the forest will be established, after which this chapter will proceed on to discuss its place in the cosmology of Arda. This exposition will be accomplished by analysing the powers and divine forces involved with this domain, specifically their genesis and teleology. The chapter will conclude with a critical assessment of the essence of the forest as an existential scene in Tolkien's legendarium.

The Forests of Middle-earth

The forest is a case of scenery constituted eminently by a concentration of trees. For Tolkien, trees are a privileged image of the force and beauty of the living and the natural, as opposed to the power and manipulation of the artificial. The servants of Evil are always enemies of the trees, such as is the case of Saruman in *The Lord of the Rings* (Romero Tabares, 2004, pp. 151–152). Forests are places made of trees; yet Tolkien's treatment of the forest is different from his treatment of the individual tree. This is shown through the common structure that underlies the stories that occur within forests and the role that they play in the plot of the story and the life trajectory of the protagonists.

All forays into a Tolkien forest present these constants:

1. a sense of danger: before its appearance in the story, the forest is anticipated through warnings;

2. a paralellism with entering the underground: darkness or shadow, oppression, silence or deafness, references to 'under' or 'below';

3. the perception of the space as immense and filled with conscious, vigilant presences;

4. the distortion (perceptual or factual) of time and space;

5. a state of deprivation and helplessness: hunger, thirst, or blindness;

6. the abnormal behaviour of nature: proprotion (eg age and size), features (eg colours), water as enchantment, inversion of predation or hunt, movement of what should not move, speech in what should not speak, etc;

7. the blurring of the limits, forms and borders of reality, being a mixture of opposites: sleep–vigil, dream–vision, past–present, memory–future, natural–enchanted, right–wrong, good–evil, life–death, etc;

8. the presence of music and song;

9. the abandoning of a path into the world of the non-visible.;

10. the encounter with queer creatures: strange animals, monsters or wonderful beings; and

11. the overcoming of an experience similar to death, resulting in a vital transformation and the acquisition of a virtue (a weapon, a trait, knowledge, etc). Life as it was lived before this experience is lost forever, casting the adventurer out of the path proportional to their life into one more profoundly involved with the cosmic order.

Crossing the forests breaks the pace and cadence of the established narrative, turning it into a fairy–horror story for a short time. Altogether, the forest is presented as a location that is in a state of exception from the rest of the world, a place that is not completely in this sphere and that borders on a very different one: a liminal space. Let us consider now some actual cases.

Mirkwood

The episode in this darkened forest in *The Hobbit* is decisive in the life-path of Bilbo. It establishes, as well, a turning point in the darkening of the novel. Despite the many obstacles and enemies overcome by the protagonists up to that moment, entering Mirkwood is presented to us as a much more dangerous path than the one left behind. Crossing it will entail a sudden change in the character of Bilbo who, aware of it (Tolkien, 1999, p. 146), will transform from being dragged by circumstance to being an engine of action from now on, making him an equal to Gandalf and Thorin. The experience of the forest enables the rebirth of Bilbo from an average hobbit into an evil-fighting hero who will never be able to return to his previous life.

This forest is presented to readers through the effusive warnings against it from Beorn and Gandalf, but the chapter devoted to Mirkwood begins with the action of entering it. This is described as going underground and is openly compared with it (ibid., pp. 132–133): 'the entrance to the path was like a sort of arch leading in to a gloomy tunnel', 'soon the light at the gate was like a little bright hole far behind', 'they grew to hate the forest as heartily as they had hated the tunnels of the goblins', 'they were sick for a sight of the sun and of the sky'.

The place is described as a 'down under', suffocating space. All the more so since Mirkwood is still, thick, dark, and no less silent than the actual underground: 'the quiet was so deep that their feet seemed to thump along' (ibid., p. 132), 'and it was everlastingly still and dark and stuffy' (Ibid., p. 133). Such a place is not closed up like a tunnel, however, and its darkness is chronicled as wide and with a sentient presence: 'all the trees leaned over them and listened' (ibid., p. 132). It is said to be inhabited by wild things that are 'dark, queer, and savage' (ibid., p. 125) that remain invisible or are only hinted into sight (ibid., p. 132): 'he could catch glimpses of them whisking off the path and scuttling behind tree-trunks. There were queer noises too [...] but what made the noises he could not see'. Strange animals, monsters, dangerous beautiful elves and the Necromancer in the south (ibid., p. 130).

It is hard to measure the passing of time, and the forest does not seem to have a physical end: 'it seemed to offer even less hope of any ending' (ibid., p. 133). A time spent in permanent hunger and thirst, and beyond the hope of receiving help from Gandalf for the first time in the story.

The natural elements look and behave abnormally in the forest. Such irregularities include the colour of the animals, the water that conjures sleep and oblivion, and the proportions of size (eg spiders) and age (eg elves, trees). Similarly, the encounters that occur, wonderful or terrible, are endowed with a dreamlike aura (eg the white deer, the feast) and perceived as more threatening than regular danger. 'Sometimes there was singing in the distance too [...] And the singing was beautiful, but it sounded eerie and strange [...] they hurried on from those parts with what strength they had left' (ibid., p. 138).

The boundaries of everyday life become blurred, confusing present with memory, sleep and wake ('"It looks as if my dreams were coming true," gasped Bombur', ibid., 142), and life with death. '"A feast would be no good, if we never got back alive from it," said Thorin. "But without a feast we shan't remain alive much longer anyway," said Bombur"' (ibid., p. 142).

Before departing, Gandalf insists three times that the adventurers do not abandon the path (ibid., pp. 130–131). In Mirkwood, leaving the path of the road means to get lost in such a way that no one 'will ever see you again' (ibid., p. 130); it means moving into the world of the unseen.

Crossing this forest is in no way dissimilar to the hero's journey through the underworld that is coded into the mythologeme of the labyrinth. This is manifested in that the experience catalyses a radical transformation in Bilbo: 'Somehow [after] the killing of this giant spider [...] he felt a different person, and much fiercer and bolder [...]' (ibid., p. 146). This rebirth is matched by how the dwarves have to be rescued from a state similar to death. In addition, Bilbo obtains a marvellous weapon: Sting.

The Old Forest

Everything said about Mirkwood applies to the presentation of the Old Forest by Merry, being perilous, aware, queer, abnormal, and as if it did not quite belong in this world:

> But the Forest is queer. Everything in it is very much more alive, more aware of what is going on [...] all the trees were whispering to each other, [...] and the branches swayed and groped without any wind. They do say the trees do actually move, and can surround strangers and hem them in. [...] There are

various queer things living deep in the Forest [...] But something makes paths. Whenever one comes inside one finds open tracks; but they seem to shift and change from time to time in a queer fashion. (Tolkien, 2005, pp. 144–145)

This alien atmosphere had been set into the landscape since the hobbits left Crickhollow, but the forest is properly accessed through a tunnel-gate and there is a progressive darkening upon entering, often emphasised as 'down-under' (ibid., 146–147). This forest is only finally exited through the Barrowdowns, an ancient graveyard. There, the adventurers face the dead (Barrow-wrights), are almost taken by them and obtain from the experience weapons that will have great importance in the upcoming events. The description of their exit through the valley is like coming out of a tunnel (ibid., 191).

Despite their efforts, the hobbits are unable to make progress in any direction other than the path the forest seems to want them to follow, like a maze (as directly stated by Tom Bombadil, ibid., 165), guiding them to its centre, said to be from where all the queerness came (ibid., 149). There is an overall sense of vigilance on behalf of the trees (ibid., 146). This silent presence establishes the forest as an otherworld to which the lively hobbits are strangers, reduced to a helpless child-like state against the immensity around: 'As they listened, they began [...] to feel themselves as the strangers where all other things were at home' (ibid., p. 170).

In the Old Forest, nature behaves abnormally (moving paths, whispering vegetation, flesh-eating trees) and the normal boundaries between realities become blurred. Such is the case for the present and the memory of the past: 'for it was indeed ancient, a survivor of vast forgotten woods [...] remembering times when they were lords' (ibid., p. 170), '[The singing of Tom] had now wandered into strange regions beyond their memory and beyond their waking thought' (ibid., p. 171). The indistinction between sleep, wakefulness, vision and enchantment is particularly pronounced after the encounter with Old Man Willow. Such lack of discernment is also seen between the concepts of right and wrong as well as good and evil, which work differently in the world outside the forest. Examples of this blurring include the fact that Tom is master in a place where everything belongs to itself, that nature is discovered as full of hatred but there is no need to fight or destroy it, or that the One Ring does not seem to have an effect there.

There is a constant presence of song while the hobbits stay in the forest. Most of the effect of this music is described 'as if' it were enchantment; particularly when this singing comes from the disconcerting characters of Old Man Willow, Tom or Goldberry. Throughout his legendarium, Tolkien consistently describes events that could have a supernatural source in equivocal terms, particularly 'seemed' and 'as if'. This lack of precise description is heavily employed in events taking place in forests. It is, therefore, significant that in this forest we are introduced to the existence of powers and forces in Arda other than those involved in the events pertaining the ring. This is what makes the whole encounter with Tom come across as incongruous to the universe and plot in which he makes such a striking appearance.

Fangorn

The Old Forest takes us to Fangorn, for both used to be the same forest in ancient times. But while the Old Forest is characterised as full of 'pride and rooted wisdom, and with malice' (ibid., p. 170), Fangorn is, in the words of Legolas, watchful and angry; it is a place 'old and full of memory' (Tolkien, 2007. p. 640). In *The Two Towers*, all travellers that enter this forest are tired and short of provisions. The first thing that the narration tells us about this forest is that: 'A queer stifling feeling came over them, as if the air were too thin or too scanty for breathing. [...] the trees that stood silently about them, rank upon rank, until they faded away into grey twilight in every direction' (ibid., p. 560).

Again, there is an action of going under and moving into a huge, dark space within which the hobbits are unable to orientate themselves; the first sensation experienced by each is of being lost. The place is described as 'dim' and 'stuffy' (ibid., p. 560), still, untidy and untouched by time. It is compared to Mirkwood by Merry and Gimli (ibid., pp. 601, 640) in its undeniable link to darkness. A darkness imbued into the beings that inhabit it, like the Huorns, of which it is said that 'they seem able to wrap themselves in shadow' (ibid., p. 737).

Fangorn can change not only its interior paths but its very location, such as during the Battle of Helm's Deep, in which those who entered the forest were never seen again: 'Wailing they passed under the waiting shadow of the trees; and from that shadow none ever came again' (ibid., p. 707). In addition to this most unnatural characteristic of being a mobile forest, other abnormal features of this area include talking trees and water with the virtue to provide immediate physical growth.

This forest is the dwelling place of primal creatures of explicit ambivalence, such as the Ents or the Huorns, who are not defined by the moral boundaries that govern the world outside the woodland. This otherness is expressed primarily through the notions of queerness, wildness, and danger or perilousness (eg, ibid., pp. 627, 737). These aspects are often mistaken for evil due to the fact that they are, in many instances, shown combined with anger, darkness and danger. They could not be farther from it, however, as is directly stated by Legolas, 'I do not think the wood feels evil, whatever tales may say' (ibid., p. 639) and by Gandalf, 'and Fangorn himself, he is perilous too; yet he is wise and kindly nonetheless' ibid., p. 651).

Considering the context, this forest is the logical scene for the equivocal first encounter of the protagonists with two Maiar: Saruman in disguise and Gandalf who was brought back from dead with a changed shape, identity and memories. This situational framework does not allow the adventurers to distinguish good from evil, safety from danger, friend from foe, dark from luminous, or presence from memory. This indistinction between the limits of things is also made explicit as confusion between sleep and wake experienced by the Ents (ibid., p. 609).

There is a very important presence of music and songs in the speech of Treebeard that, despite their appearance as ditties, convey arcane information. This ancient context, available to the reader of *The Silmarillion*, elucidates on how the introduction of the Fangorn Forest to the story broadens the scope of the events narrated in *The Lord of the Rings* from a political war into a cosmic event. What is being fought here is not a certain political order but a universal force; therefore, the natural world itself becomes involved. This is one of the main elements that provide a crucial insight into how the ambiguity that the natural world demonstrates to men and even elves is not aligned with evil.

The events related to Fangorn, particularly the scene of the Ents marching into battle, are some of the most eloquent examples concerning how the landscapes of Middle-earth are active agents in the actions that occur in them, including the spiritual ones.

Nan Elmoth

This forest is the most ancient of the examples presented here and the only one presented from an elven perspective. This is the forest in which Elwë-Thingol found the Maia Melian. There is no forewarning of danger but, like other woodlands, this area is defined by a nocturnal quality. Rather than filled with an oppressive darkness, however, this forest is 'starlit' (Tolkien, 2001, p. 55); this difference may be because the narration is given from the perspective of an elf. There is a meaningful contraposition between light and darkness in the whole passage that is resolved through a darkening and an explicit disproportion: 'the trees of Nan Elmoth grew tall and dark before they spoke any word' (ibid., p. 55). In this forest the trees grew to be the tallest and darkest in Beleriand, blocking the sun entirely from the forest floor (ibid., p. 132).

Elwë entered Nan Elmoth led by the song of nightingales and 'an enchantment fell on him' (ibid., p. 55) that set him apart from his peers, leading him into a different state of being. The transition happens through the action of going 'under the shadows' of the trees. The enchantment acts through a music that leads to forgottenness, silence and to the loss of the path: 'He forgot then utterly all his people and all the purposes of his mind, and following the birds under the shadow of the trees he passed deep into Nan Elmoth and was lost.' (ibid., p. 55)

This going astray will result in the wonderful encounter with Melian, a Power that belongs to the Otherworld; this convergence is defined by the action of Elwë of coming 'out from the darkness' (Ibid, p. 56). The consequence of the incident is that the elf, in stillness and silence, is removed from the normal course of space and time, being impossible to find by his former companions and thought dead. Upon his awakening from the spell, as if reborn, he would take a new name and, receiving Melian and her great power, he became one of the highest monarchs presented in *The Silmarillion*.

Moreover, this change is true of Melian as well. Her encounter with Elwë is equally unexpected and she is existentially shaken. Precisely because she is one of the Powers, the transforming value of this experience is more profoundly explicit, leading her out of the path proportional to her life and transforming her existence. Afterwards, she became the only being among all the Ainur to adopt the true form of the Sons of Ilúvatar and to give birth, never again returning to Valinor (the Otherworld).

Lothlórien

This case study has been left for last because it displays two peculiarities, setting it apart from the other locations. This region retains the image of forests from before the Marring of Arda, 'on the land of Lórien there was no stain' (Tolkien, 2005, p. 456). Additionally, Lothlórien is the only example of woodlands endowed of a solar-diurnal quality. In spite of these remarkable differences, venturing into these woods still entails the same phenomenology for the adventurer but under a different aspect, for here is added the danger of eucathastrophic liminality: one not established through harm and suffering but through joy and delight.

In this episode is found: an arrival at the forest in the dark and in a state of deprivation (ibid., 439), a parallel between entering it and going into Moria (ibid., 440), warnings about the forest before entering it (ibid., p. 440), difficulty in differentiating danger from evil (ibid., p. 440), the presence of enchanted-singing water (ibid., 441), forgottenness (ibid., p. 441), the inability to orient oneself (ibid., pp. 452–453), the indiscernibility of opposites, and so forth. All of these events, which result in the vital expansion of the adventurers and the obtaining of gifts, are experienced, however, with joy and with the lucidity that parting from it will be more devastating than any evil. 'Torment in the dark was the danger that I feared, and it did not hold me back. But I would not have come, had I known the danger of light and joy.' (ibid., p. 493)

The Cosmic Functionality of the Forest

In *The Silmarillion*, *The Hobbit* and *The Lord of the Rings*, we are presented with two kinds of forests. The regular woodlands of Middle-earth, like the rest of Arda, are marred by Melkor. Contrastingly, in Lothlórien, the virtue of Galadriel pushed the marring away, allowing the land to grow in semblance to the primal forests. In all examples, however, it is possible to establish the experiential framework detailed at the beginning of the chapter.

It has been demonstrated that the forests of Arda are places where reality is altered by the intermingling of another order of being. They operate as an existential threshold that allows an encounter outside of normality that profoundly alters the lives of its protagonists. This is indicated by the markers of: darkness and shadow, danger and wildness, dream and vision, the indistinction of categories and their redefinition, enchantment, and nocturnality (except for Lóthlorien). Such liminality establishes the scope of the cosmic functionality of the forest that reflects the constitution of the cosmology developed by Tolkien.

The approach developed here is based on the recognition that the cosmology built by Tolkien constitutes an autonomous mythical world. It is self-consistent in its physical and metaphysical laws, which are devised and developed through an efficient cause (that which produces an effect by a causal process) and a teleological cause (purpose, directive principle or goal). This foundation binds the diverse stories of Middle-earth into a coherent whole. The use of this device enables a solid ontological reflection upon many concepts that Tolkien never explained without having to resort to external causes (imitation, influences of the author, etc.).

In order to fully appreciate the role of the forest in Arda, it is necessary to comprehend the powers and divine forces involved with this domain. These entities are the Ainur, which are personal metaphysical forces born from the mind of Eru (God). They moulded, nurture and sustain the world, following a vision inspired by Eru. Therefore, every aspect of reality refers to one or more of these forces as their origin or manager, with the exception of the creation of personal entities (men and elves), which Eru reserves for himself.

Within these forces there is a distinction of categories, which is not based in might or power, but in authority, majesty and reverence: on one hand, we have the Valar ('the powers'), on the other, the Maiar ('the beautiful'). Another distinction can be made among the Valar; eight of them are the Aratar ('The Exalted'), who surpass in majesty the other six Valar but who are all equal among each other in reverence. These figures are related to each other through ties of kinship, marriage and servitude.

The structure presented is one of great eloquence. Considering the architecture of this universe, this research found it fruitful to conduct an analysis of the arrangement of the Ainur by employing the same methods that are applied to the study of historical mythologies. Mainly the one proposed by the Karl Kerényi (Kerényi, 1979, p. 3–4) will be taken as a reference

Accordingly, the personal bonds of the Ainur should be understood such that marital unions show a confluence of the spheres of power of each deity, meaning that two different aspects of reality are wed attending to *sense* and *purpose*. The bond between parents and children serves to show the nature of the parents from a new perspective or through a specific relation. Tolkien's evolution in his conception of the metaphysical nature of the Eä (creation) soon led him to decide against reproduction among the Ainur, but this is replaced in identical terms by relations of vassalage with the Maiar. Therefore, the Valar must be looked at as the structural powers that establish the world. These forces create spheres of reality, each according to the nature and interests of each Vala. The Maiar are these forces under a particular aspect, relation or action.

A clear example of this structure is found in the Vala Ulmo, lord of the waters and the depths. Ulmo is described as indomitable, profoundly loving, and his song retains an echo of the primal music by which the universe was made. He is unwed, but we are told of three Maiar that serve him: Uinen, Ossë and Salmar. Uinen embodies all benignant and nurturing aspects of water. She is kind and loving; she cares for all sea creatures and sailors. Furthermore, she is the only force with power over Ossë (establishing a hierarchy of kindness), to whom she is wed. Ossë embodies the wild, violent and dangerous aspects of water. The only information that is known of Salmar is that he devised the instruments used to make the music of the sea. It is clear how, even though they are each different characters, these Maiar are all aspects of Ulmo's sphere of power. They are aspects of water as a power of the world.

Regarding the internal hierarchy among the Valar themselves, the Aratar are structural forces, being aspects of the world constituent of it, without which the world would not exist or would be entirely different. The other Valar are fundamental powers of the world, which enrich and complement the structural ones by relying on them. This action manifests with particular clarity in the bonds of siblinghood among the Ainur.

Each power takes realisation in the world at a double level: physical and spiritual, which are interdependent and simultaneous. Among the Aratar, a subdivision can also be distinguished that inscribes their spheres of power. Firstly, those that belong to the natural constitution of the world: Ulmo as indomitability, Aulë as plasticity, Yavanna as vitality, Oromë as death. Lastly, those that belong to its supernatural composition: Manwë as hope, Varda as grace, Mandos as justice, Nienna as mercy.

Relevant to the sphere of forests are Yavannä, Oromë, Vána, and the Maiar Tilion, Melian, Aiwendil-Radagast, and indirectly Estë and Lorien. Yavanna is the designer and ruler of all living nature. She is known to be particularly fond of trees but, rather than forests, she makes pastures her home. Vána is the younger sister of Yavanna. This concept of relational age expresses that Vána's sphere of power depends on that of her sister and, indeed, Vána is the exuberance of the living nature her sister enables. She dwells in gardens, but she often goes to the forests of Oromë, a border between the pastures of Yavanna and the lands of Ungoliant, a place of great danger and darkness.

Oromë is Vána's spouse, which indicates a complementarity (a shared sense) between both spheres of power. He is the Ainu with a fuller connection with the forest, not as its *maker* but as its *dweller*. The creation of the forest is Yavanna's work but life in the forest is Oromë's realm and, therefore, forests and their creatures are considered his domain. Oromë is an Aratar, one of the structural natural powers, and his realm is the hunt. His contribution to the world is to wander the forests hunting, which is bringing death to living creatures. This duty is not a consequence of the corruption of Arda by Melkor, being an act of restoration (as is the case of Tulkas). It is true that, after the marring, Oromë hunts monsters and fell creatures that dwell in dark forests but he was already the power of the hunt when the world was pure. This fact raises a question about what this 'hunting' is that is structural to the world.

Oromë performs several meaningful tasks while in the course of his hunting activities. He is the first one to find the elves when they awake in Cuiviénen, a land near the Wild Wood. He names the race of the elves and, in the *Lhammas*, we are told that Oromë teaches them how to speak (the Oromeian languages). He acts as a messenger between Middle-earth and Valinor (the Otherworld). Furthermore, in earlier versions of the legendarium, he devises the Ilweran, the rainbow bridge that allows travelling between Valinor and Middle-earth. Additionally, Oromë is the one who shows the elves the path to Valinor. All of these attributes are typical characterisations of a psychopomp deity, being a guide that moves freely between *this* and the *other* world, providing passage for souls and knowledge. Examples of other such gods include: Anubis, Hermes, Charun, Ganesh or the Valkyries. This combined information leads to the conclusion that Oromë is a God of Death, specifically of natural death. Furthermore, the confluence between death and the exuberance of living nature that is seen in the marriage between Oromë and Vána is common in mythology; well-known examples of this being the Greek god Dionysus or the marriage between Persephone and Hades

Popular interpretation assigns this role to Mandos. Mandos, however, does not manage death but the dead. This role is within his domain because his sphere of power is justice; he is not involved in the processes or experiences of the transit between life and death.

Therefore, in Arda, the Lord of the Forests is the deity of death. This places him among the many traditions that link great hunts or wild hunts with the passing of souls to the Otherworld. The hunting theme is present in the woodlands listed above in varying degrees of explicitness: 'And as they sat it seemed that they could hear the noise of a great hunt going by the north of the path, though they saw no sign of it' (Tolkien, 1999. p. 137).

The above demonstrates that the forests of Tolkien act as a liminal space between the world of the living and the world of death. These places, full of enchantment, are where one can easily slip into one realm or the other, where things from beyond can be present. It is, therefore, pertinent to remember that in Tolkien's legendarium death is neither evil nor a consequence of evil but, rather, to men it is a gift. Yet, like all things of the world, the woodlands were corrupted by the evil of Melkor and, thus, forests are the chosen scene of encounters with most monsters (especially nameless ones) and creatures that hunt down and bring death to people. These actions present themselves as if in mockery of the works of Oromë, occurring as a disgrace, as an evil. Consequently, Oromë's action as a hunter of monsters in the marred Arda is that of the psychopomp protecting the ways to the Otherworld. Additionally, for this liminal character it why woodlands are thresholds to otherworldly wonder, which can be even more devastating than disgrace.

The Moon

The explicit interpretation of Oromë as Lord of Death is necessary in order to establish the role of the Maiar who are linked to forests, Tilion being the most prevalent of these beings. Tilion was a hunter in the service of Oromë. This service, under the analysis posited above, should be understood as an aspect of the sphere of power of Oromë in action. Tilion is the Maiar that became the moon. There is abundant material on the relationship between the moon and the forests, most of which are characterised by a nocturnal quality.

Discussing the respective action of the lights of the moon and the sun in the events of Tolkien's work deviates far from the theme of this chapter. It is noteworthy, however, how the light of the moon shows the virtue of transmuting the darkness associated with evil into a shadow that allows a visionary and restorative experience, intermingling the visible and the invisible. The moon is linked to the same darkness that is brought about by the shade of the trees. This darkness does not deny light, but is the consequence of concealment or shelter. Such darkness is of Lórien and Estë, which allows relief, rest, visions, and the enchantment of the Otherworld. Likewise, the moon has a prominent presence in all those events in which the forces of nature take action in the fight against evil; such is the case of the defeat of Isengard by the Ents (Tolkien, 2007, p. 745).

Therefore, in the narrative action of the light of the moon, an effect of the cosmic force governed by Oromë is elucidated. This is shown in the establishment of liminal spaces, in its connection to wild nature and in its eminent presence in the slaying of evil creatures.

Conclusion

Comparative mythology, following the works of Joseph Campbell (Campbell, 1972), demonstrates that one of the most relevant liminal scenes is the mytheme of the journey through the Otherworld. Tolkien includes this narrative structure in his work but, in coherence with the rules of the universe he created, this liminality corresponds to the forest and not to the underworld. This performance is attested through Oromë's surprising cosmological role as lord of beasts, traveller between realms of existence, donor of hidden knowledge, fierce enemy of evil and minister of natural death among the exuberance of life.

In Tolkien's works, the woodlands act as the geographical marker of *something else that is not seen*. Wonders and deadly things dwell in these spaces, shrouded by the shadow of the trees and veiled in moonlight. In forests, the existence of the wanderer is put into a threshold state and confronted with everything that is *other* to it. This experience results in an existential stir that makes it impossible for the wanderers to return to their previous life as they have passed into a new way of living more intimately concerned with the higher order of the world.

This profound change becomes concrete in an expansion and enrichment of the characters' existential space: of their identity, courage, aspirations, beliefs and desires. Above all, their understanding of the world deepens to beyond what is seen, known and experienced by men, elves and even the Ainur.

Bibliography

Campbell, J. (1972), *El héroe de las mil caras: Psicoanálisis del mito*, Mexico: Fondo de Cultura Económica.

Kereìnyi, K. (1979), *Goddesses of Sun and Moon*, Texas: Spring Publications.

Kereìnyi, K. (2006), *En el laberinto*, Madrid, Siruela.

Romero Tabares, I. (2004), *En el corazoìn del mito: la dimensioìn espiritual de "El senÞor de los anillos"*, Madrid: PPC.

Ronnberg, A. & Martin, K. (2011), *El libro de los siìmbolos: reflexiones sobre las imaìgenes arquetiìpicas*, Ko¨ln: Taschen.

Tolkien, J.R.R. (1999), *The Hobbit, or There and Back Again*, London, Harper Collins.

Tolkien, J.R.R. (2001), *The Silmarillion*, Boston: Mariner Books/Houghton Mifflin Harcourt.

Tolkien, J.R.R. (2005), *The Fellowship of the Ring*, London: Harper Collins.

Tolkien, J.R.R. (2007), *The Two Towers* [ebook], London: Harper Collins.

Chapter 9

The Fiendish Forests of Middle-earth: Tolkien's Trees as Ominous Adversaries

Damian O'Byrne

There are no trees like the trees of that land

The Lord of the Rings

On 9 August 1973, Michael Tolkien took a photograph of his grandfather leaning against a huge black pine tree in Oxford University's Botanic Garden. The tree was one hundred and seventy-four years old, supposedly having been planted in 1799 from a seed collected in Austria. During his time in Oxford, Michael's grandfather, an author, had grown incredibly fond of the tree, often writing beneath it, naming it Laocoon[*] and, so the story goes, becoming inspired to create his race of ents – huge anthropomorphic trees – by this single black pine. What Michael Tolkien could not have known at the time, was that his grandfather would die less than a month later and that this would be the last known photograph ever taken of J.R.R. Tolkien. Of course, quite how much of the inspirational power of this tree has been romanticised by history is hard to say, but the black pine was definitely a favourite of Tolkien and, in the years since his death, the tree became colloquially know as Tolkien's Tree. It is perhaps appropriate that the last known photograph of Tolkien shows him touching a tree, given that a love of nature and trees in particular profoundly influenced the creation of his Middle-earth stories for almost sixty years.

J.R.R. Tolkien made no secret of his love of trees; he wrote in a 1955 letter, 'I am (obviously) much in love with plants and above all trees, and always have been; and I find human mistreatment of them as hard to bear as some find ill-treatment of animals' (Carpenter, 2006, Letter 165). In his biography of Tolkien, Humphrey Carpenter wrote that 'he liked most of all to be *with* trees. He would climb them, lean against them, even talk to them' (Carpenter, 2016: 38). Tolkien's preoccupation with trees is immediately obvious to anyone who has encountered his Middle-earth legendarium and his major

[*]   In Greek and Roman myth, Laocoön was a Trojan priest who was killed by sea serpents – the way in which the thick round branches of the black pine intertwine with one another resembles a mass of sea serpents.

works, *The Hobbit* (1937), *The Lord of the Rings* (1954–55), and *The Silmarillion* (1977) are packed full of trees and forests; the forested realms of Doriath and Dorthonion are major locations in *The Silmarillion*; Thorin's Company spend two months under the boughs of the vast forest of Mirkwood in *The Hobbit*; finally, the Fellowship travels through no less than three forests in the first half of *The Lord of the Rings*.

Tolkien's fascination with trees makes it all but impossible to read his work without the feeling that there is an underlying moral or message, a message that is most frequently suggested to be a critique of the consequences of industrialisation. Joe Kraus argued that 'as someone who loved nature, it troubled Tolkien to see the reckless and unplanned development of much of the countryside that he knew' (2004, p. 141). In *The Lord of the Rings*, this 'reckless and unplanned development' is perhaps most commonly argued to be personified by Saruman, the treacherous wizard who destroys vast swathes of the forest of Fangorn to further his own selfish needs.

While such overt interpretations are appealing, it is dangerous to attempt to identify too much of Tolkien's world view in the text given that he frequently criticised allegory and claimed that *The Lord of the Rings* was 'not about JRRT at all, and it is at no point an attempt to allegorise his experience of life' (Carpenter, 2006, Letter 183). For Tolkien at least, the fact that his works are overflowing with references to trees and forests does not, *alone*, prove that he regarded them with any special affinity and in fact he wrote in 1956 that there was 'no "allegory", moral, political, or contemporary in the work at all' (Carpenter, 2006, Letter 181).

However, even if we accept that Tolkien's Middle-earth betrays little of his world-view by way of direct allegory, his letters, first published in 1981, offer a fascinating insight into what was clearly a very personal and protective love of trees. In a 1962 letter, he recounts the history of a single tree he remembers from his youth:

> There was a great tree – a huge poplar with vast limbs – visible through my window even as I lay in bed. I loved it, and was anxious about it. It had been savagely mutilated some years before, but had gallantly grown new limbs – though of course not with the unblemished grace of its former natural self; and now a foolish neighbour was agitating to have it felled. Every tree has its enemy, few have an advocate. Too often the hate is irrational, a fear of anything large and alive, and not easily tamed or destroyed ... Any wind that could have uprooted it and hurled it on her house, would have demolished her and her house without any assistance from the tree. I believe it still stands where it did. Though many winds have blown since (Carpenter, 2006, Letter 241).

Two years later, in the foreword to *Tree and Leaf*, Tolkien once more recalled the same poplar, writing:

> One of [*Tree and Leaf's*] sources was a great limbed poplar tree that I could see even lying in bed. It was suddenly lopped and mutilated by its owner, I do not

know why. It is cut down now, a less barbarous punishment for any crimes it may have been accused of, such as being large and alive. I do not think it has any friends, or any mourners except myself and a pair of owls (Tolkien, 2001, p. vi).

In these passages, Tolkien describes how trees can have 'friends', 'enemies' and be 'loved' 'gallant' 'mutilated' and 'punished' – fully anthropomorphising them and revealing a very personal love of trees. It is particularly interesting to see that two years later he recalls the fate of the tree very differently; whether or not this is a simple mistake in one of the texts or a later admission of an unfortunate truth is unclear but perhaps it is inevitable that such a deep-rooted and passionate love for trees would find its way into his writing, even if not as direct allegory.

Over the course of the first half of *The Lord of the Rings*, Saruman, a wizard who has 'left the path of wisdom' (Tolkien, 1995, p. 252), devastates the trees from Fangorn Forest to fuel the industrial fires of his fortress of Isengard, leaving 'wastes of stump and bramble where once there were singing groves' (Tolkien, 1995, p. 463). It is commonly argued by more journalistic texts that Saruman's destruction of Fangorn is an overt analogy for the slow ruination of the English countryside; a quick *Google* search reveals countless articles with titles like '*Isengard Represented the Industrial Revolution: Because Tolkien Hated Technology*'.

However, again, such simplistic allegorical interpretations are somewhat at odds with Tolkien's firm insistence, reiterated in the 1965 foreword to the second edition of *The Lord of the Rings*, that the story does not have 'any allegorical significance or contemporary political reference whatsoever' (Tolkien, 1995, p. xvii). Of course, the abundance of forests planted within Tolkien's legendarium certainly deserves critical investigation and Tolkien did admit that 'there is a "moral", I suppose, in any tale worth telling' (Carpenter, 2006, Letter 109) so it would be foolish to assume that the frequent use of trees in his work bore no significance. However, rather than a simple allegory about industrialisation, I believe that the 'moral worth telling' in Tolkien's work is that nature is a sentient, violent and vengeful force that will strike back against those who attack it.

Great shadows fell across them; trunks and branches of trees hung dark and threatening over the path

The Lord of the Rings

The forests of Middle-earth possess a dark agency of their own; they are malevolent places where paths 'shift and change from time to time in queer fashion' (Tolkien, 1995: 108) and in which the characters can feel 'the ill will of the wood pressing on them' (Tolkien, 1995, p. 110). In *The Silmarillion*, the forest of Taur-nu-Fuin is described as:

A region of such dread and dark enchantment that even the Orcs would not enter it unless need drove them... the Trees that grew there after the burning were black and grim, and their roots were tangled, groping in the dark like claws; and those who strayed among them became lost and blind, and were strangled or pursued to madness by phantoms of terror (Tolkien, 2002, p. 180).

Rumours of the dangers of the forests of Middle-earth spread far and wide and the heroes of Tolkien's stories are frequently warned in advance about the forests through which they must pass; In *The Hobbit*, Beorn warns Thorin's Company that in the forest of Mirkwood, 'the wild things are dark, queer and savage' (Tolkien, 2012, p. 166), while in *The Lord of the Rings*, the hobbits have barely started their adventure when they must pass through The Old Forest which is described in hobbit legend as 'a dark bad place if half the tales be true' (Tolkien, 1995, p. 22).* Later in their journey, our heroes are warned not to 'risk becoming entangled' in either Fangorn forest or the woods of Lothlórien, for they are 'strange' and 'queer' places (Tolkien, 1995, pp. 364/456). One of these warnings carries even more weight given that it is given by an ent – one of the huge tree-like creatures supposedly inspired by Tolkien's Tree in Oxford – in Middle-earth, even the trees warn you about the trees. Time and time again, the forests of Middle-earth are positioned as mysterious, dangerous and perilous places and certainly not passive, peaceful woodland to be easily harvested for the fires of industry.

Of course, the concept of forests as dangerous places, full of peril and malevolent creatures, is nearly as old as the forests themselves and certainly not unique to Middle-earth. Tolkien's forests of Mirkwood, Fangorn and Taur-nu-Fuin are simply modern extensions of the countless forests of ancient myths and legends. There are numerous parallels between Tolkien's Middle-earth and the fairy tales collected by the Brothers Grimm in both plot** and the use of forests as a perilous setting; Snow White finds herself 'all alone in the great forest' (Grimm, 2006, p. 251) and when Hansel and Gretel are captured by the evil witch they are lost in the forest 'where it is the thickest' (Grimm, 2006, p. 86).

In *Snow White and the Seven Dwarfs*, Disney's animated adaptation of the Grimm brothers' tale, Snow White becomes lost in a forest in which she seems to be 'pursued to madness by phantoms of terror' and the trees attack her with arms 'groping in the dark like claws'. The narrative implies that these are primarily hallucinations but they perfectly match Tolkien's description of Taur-nu-Fuin and, in a film populated by dwarves and evil queens, the idea of a genuinely haunted forest does not seem so unlikely. In another unlikely coincidence, both *The Hobbit* and *Snow White and the Seven*

---

*   This warning comes on page two of *The Lord of the Rings*, the dangers of the forests of Middle-earth being highlighted from the very beginning of the story.

**   Tolkien's story of *Beren and Lúthien* contains clear echoes of Rapunzel when Luthien, imprisoned 'as high as men could fashion' (Tolkien, 2017: 53); in Hirilorn, the 'Queen of Trees', lengthens her hair using magic and casts out 'her long hair from the window... [and climbs] down that rope of hair' (Tolkien, 2017: 56).

Dwarfs, two fairy tale-like stories concerning the adventures of a band of dwarves in a haunted forest, were released in 1937 and perhaps both helped to re-establish the idea of the dangers of the forest for a new generation.

Further parallels between the forests of fairy tales and Middle-earth can be found in the warnings given to those entering the woods, with Beorn's advice to Thorin's Company that they must not leave the path 'for any reason' (Tolkien, 2012:166) echoing the warning given to Little Red Cap to 'not run off the path' (Grimm, 2006: 139). Nevertheless, despite the warnings both Little Red Cap and Thorin's Company are enticed away from path, by the wolf and the elves of Mirkwood respectively, and only narrowly avoid disaster in the process.

However, what sets the forests of Middle-earth apart from the wolf and witch-infested forests of ancient fairy tales is that what makes them so queer and perilous is not some form of monster lurking in the forest, but rather the sentient power of the trees themselves.

None were more dangerous than the great Willow: his heart was rotten

The Lord of the Rings

The Lord of the Rings tells the story of Frodo, Sam, Pippin and Merry, four hobbits who go on an epic journey to destroy a ring that has the power to bring about the end of the world. However, before the hobbits have even left their homeland they become lost in the Old Forest and the first real threat to their lives* comes from Old Man Willow – a tree. Old Man Willow is a willow tree who lives at the heart of the Old Forest, 'the queerest part of the whole wood – the centre from which all the queerness comes' (Tolkien, 1995, p. 111) and represents the first but by no means the last example of a tree that can think and feel in *The Lord of the Rings*. Tolkien himself once drew an illustration of Old Man Willow in which the folds in the bark give the appearance of eyes and it is quite clear that there is an evil spirit living within the tree. Tolkien writes that:

> His heart was rotten, but his strength was green; and he was cunning... His grey thirsty spirit drew power out of the earth and spread like fine root-threads in the ground, and invisible twig-fingers in the air, till it had under its dominion nearly all the trees of the Forest (Tolkien, 1995, p. 128).

As soon as the four hobbits enter Old Man Willow's domain, a hypnotic spell seems to be cast on them:

> Sleepiness seemed to be creeping out of the ground and up their legs, and falling softly on the air upon their heads and eyes ... it seemed that they could

---

*   They have encountered the mysterious black riders by this point but Old Man Willow represents the first overt attempt to kill them.

almost hear words, cool words, saying something about water and sleep… the leaves rustled and whispered, but with a sound now of faint and far-off laughter (Tolkien, 1995, pp. 114–115).

The hobbits find themselves lying down almost involuntarily and, once they have fallen asleep, Old Man Willow attempts to *consume* them. Sam returns to his senses just in time to witness 'a great tree-root… holding [Frodo] down' (Tolkien, 1995, p. 115) and, when Sam has saved him, Frodo confirms that 'the beastly tree' (Tolkien, 1995. p. 115) *threw* him in the river. As Frodo and Sam look for their friends, it transpires that Old Man Willow has already devoured Merry and Pippin and Merry screams from inside that 'he' (Tolkien, 1995, p. 116) has threatened to squeeze him in two.

Tolkien revealed in a 1972 letter that the trees of the Old Forest were 'hostile to two legged creatures because of the memory of many injuries… [and that] in all my works I take the part of trees as against all their enemies' (Carpenter, 2006, Letter 339), implying that it was years of torment by the free peoples of Middle-earth that had caused Old Man Willow to seek vengeance on the hobbits. Old Man Willow is a sentient and resentful creature, consumed with rage at centuries of mistreatment and willing to do anything do ensure his own survival; Tolkien's letter implied that he fully understood, if not supported, his perspective. The Old Man Willow episode is a strange and surprising sequence in the story, particularly given how early it occurs, but one which instantly tells the reader that the trees of Middle-earth are sentient beings that can be extremely dangerous.

The reason that the malevolent nature of some of Tolkien's trees is often overlooked is perhaps because the Old Man Willow scene is often excised from adaptations. Peter Jackson's film trilogy of *The Lord of the Rings* (2001–2003), Ralph Bakshi's animated *The Lord of the Rings* (1978) and the BBC's radio adaptation of *The Lord of the Rings* (1981) – almost certainly the three most popular adaptations – all omit the sequence in its entirety, perhaps because it 'does not fit with Tolkien's vision of other trees' (Flieger, 2000: 149). However, a slightly altered version of the scene is included, much later in the story's narrative, in the extended edition of Peter Jackson's *The Two Towers* (2002).* As the sequence starts, Merry and Pippin have been rescued by Treebeard, one of the oldest ents in Middle-earth, and have been temporarily left alone in Fangorn Forest. Merry realises that Pippin has been drinking enchanted water in a bid to grow taller and grabs the water, despite Pippin's warning that 'Treebeard said that you shouldn't have any, he said it could well be dangerous'. In the ensuing struggle, Merry and Pippin are suddenly attacked by a tree and the scene plays out largely as the Old Man Willow scene does in the book, with the hobbits being dragged into the heart of the tree. The scene not only introduces the concept of

---

★   *The Lord of the Rings* is made up of three books, *The Fellowship of the Ring*, *The Two Towers* and *The Return of the King*. Peter Jackson used the same names for his three film adaptations.

vicious and villainous trees to the film audience but also represents another link to the fairy tales of the Brothers Grimm and their multitude of stories concerning children lost in the forest.

Tolkien's hobbits are a cheery but physically short people (typically three to four feet in height) and their stature and temperament leads many of the characters in *The Lord of the Rings* to frequently position them as children; Aragorn tells Éomer that they would appear as 'children to your eyes' (Tolkien, 1995, p. 424) and Gandalf chastises Pippin for his childish behaviour, saying 'This is a serious journey not a hobbit walking-party' (Tolkien, 1995, p. 305). As such, it is very easy to make connections between Merry and Pippin's adventure in Mirkwood, in which two 'children', lost in a forest are nearly killed after drinking a forbidden draft, and classic fairy tales like Hansel and Gretel in which two children, lost in a forest, are nearly killed after beginning to eat the witch's house which was 'built of bread and covered with cakes' (Grimm, 2006, p. 90).

In the novel, Merry and Pippin are only saved from Old Man Willow by the timely intervention of Tom Bombadil, a colourful and complicated character who divides opinion amongst Middle-earth fans and who was also cut from the three adaptations mentioned above. In the adapted sequence in Jackson's *The Two Towers*, it is the return of Treebeard that saves Merry and Pippin, releasing the hobbits by commanding Old Man Willow to 'Eat earth, dig deep, drink water, go to sleep', the same words spoken by Bombadil in the book. Tolkien describes Treebeard, and his fellow ents, as the 'shepherds of the Trees' (Tolkien, 2002, p. 41), charged with keeping the 'bad', 'black' and 'rotten' hearts (Tolkien, 1995, pp. 457/480/572) of the more dangerous trees in check. Having first met Merry and Pippin in Fangorn Forest, the same forest that Saruman has been destroying to fuel his fires, Treebeard eventually decides to rouse the other ents to anger, leading them to attack Saruman's fortress of Isengard, removing him as a power in the storyline and thus playing a huge part in the survival of Middle-earth.

I have an odd feeling about these Ents: somehow I don't think they are quite as safe and, well, funny as they seem

The Lord of the Rings

Treebeard's protection of Merry and Pippin leads to him being commonly depicted as a friendly, grandfatherly figure and this and his part in the destruction of Isengard positions him and the other ents as being firmly on the side of good. However, the actions of this most enigmatic of Tolkien's creations become even more intriguing given that he was originally conceived as a *villain*. *The History of Middle-earth*, edited by Tolkien's son Christopher, is a twelve-volume series of books that charts the development of Tolkien's legendarium from the earliest drafts. Within volume six, *The Return of the Shadow*, can be found Tolkien's earliest ideas for the 'giant

Treebeard, who haunts the forest between the river and the south mountains [and who] pretends to be friendly, but is really in league with the enemy' (Tolkien, C. 2002a, p. 397). In this early iteration, it is Treebeard rather than Saruman who holds Gandalf prisoner in *The Fellowship of the Ring* and he who was to go on to pose an obstacle to Frodo who, at that point, was to find himself lost and alone in the forest. These ideas were written in 1939, some fifteen years before the publication of *The Fellowship of the Ring* and, of course, were eventually all but entirely removed or reworked. However, it is intriguing to see that Tolkien's first ideas for the walking trees of Middle-earth were as outright villains, a more common trope than we might first believe.

Violent, evil or possessed trees are far from unique to Middle-earth, *The Evil Dead* (Sam Raimi, 1981), contains an infamous sequence in which Ellen Sandweiss' character is raped by a tree; *Poltergeist* (Tobe Hooper, 1982) contains a scene in which an ent-like tree breaks into Oliver Robbins' character's bedroom and tries to consume him in a very similar manner to Old Man Willow; and *Harry Potter and The Chamber of Secrets* (J.K. Rowling, 1998) is the first of the Harry Potter novels to introduce the Whomping Willow, a violent tree planted in the grounds of Hogwarts that draws inspiration from Old Man Willow in both attitude and name. Given popular culture's long history of violent and aggressive trees, repositioning the ents as terrifying villains is surprisingly easy, as once the kindly personality of Treebeard is removed, the idea of a bitter, anthropomorphic tree, mad with fury is a worrying concept. Merry and Pippin articulate this feeling when they say of the ents:

> They seem slow, queer, patient, almost sad; and yet I believe they could be roused. If that happened, I would rather not be on the other side... There might be all the difference between an old cow sitting and thoughtfully chewing, and a bull charging; and the change might come suddenly (Tolkien, 1995: 470).

Then, after witnessing the ents' destruction of Isengard, Merry and Pippin go on to say:

> An angry Ent is terrifying. Their fingers, and their toes, just freeze on to rock; and they tear it up like bread-crust. It was like watching the work of great tree-roots in a hundred years, all packed into a few moments ... I thought that they had been really roused before; but I was wrong. It was staggering (Tolkien, 1995: 553–54).

Of course, Tolkien ultimately decided that Treebeard and the ents would fight for the forces of good. However, rather than fighting from a purely altruistic desire to help the other free peoples of Middle-earth, the real motivation for the ents march to war could reveal more about Tolkien than Treebeard.

Could it be that the trees of Fangorn were awake, and the forest was rising, marching over the hills to war?

The Lord of the Rings

The sequence in which the ents march on Isengard, bringing the forest of Fangorn to Saruman's doorstep, is often seen as the most overt example in *The Lord of the Rings* of nature avenging itself against the horrors of industrialisation. However, Tolkien's letters reveal a more personal reason for the inclusion of the sequence that emerged from reading Shakespeare, whom he 'disliked cordially' (Carpenter, 2006, Letter 163) in his schooldays. Tolkien was repeatedly vocal of his disdain for Shakespeare's work, citing amongst other offences the 'unforgivable part' that Shakespeare played in the 'debasement' of the word 'elves' (Carpenter, 2006, Letter 149).

However, this all pales before what Tolkien called his 'bitter disappointment and disgust' with the 'shabby' use of trees in *Macbeth* (Carpenter, 2006, Letter 163). Tolkien's disappointment originated from the scene in which Macbeth hears a prophecy that he 'shall never vanquished be until/Great Birnam Wood to high Dunsinane Hill/Shall come against him' before confidently claiming 'That will never be. Who can impress the forest, bid the tree. Unfix his earthbound root?' (Act IV, Scene 1, lines 108–12). Later in the play, it seems as though the prophecy has come true when a messenger reports, 'I looked toward Birnam, and anon methought. The wood began to move' (Act V, Scene 5, lines 32–33).

The idea of a supernatural forest marching to war fascinated Tolkien and, when it is revealed that the 'moving wood' is simply Malcolm's soldiers carrying branches to disguise their numbers, he was incredibly disappointed. Tolkien stated that 'I longed to devise a setting in which the trees might really march to war' (Carpenter, 2006, Letter 163) and Treebeard's actions in *The Two Towers* represent the realisation of that desire, not only in the attack on Isengard but also some seventy-five miles south-east, at the fortress of Helm's Deep. At the climax of the Battle of Helm's Deep, the defeated orcs turn to flee out of the valley the same way they arrived but find their way barred:

> The land had changed. Where before the green dale had lain, its grassy slopes lapping the ever-mounting hills, there now a forest loomed. Great trees, bare and silent, stood, rank on rank, with tangled bough and hoary head; their twisted roots were buried in the long green grass. Darkness was under them (Tolkien, 1995, p. 529).

Here, an entire forest made up of Huorns, those trees who have become 'queer and wild. Dangerous' (Tolkien, 1995, p. 551), has marched to Helm's Deep and, to quote *Macbeth*, 'come against' the orcs. This sequence fully realises Tolkien's image of Birnam Wood and demonstrates that the actions of the ents are perhaps driven as much by the author's Shakespearian wish-fulfilment as they are by the ents' moral desire to help others. However, even if we overlook the fact that the ents could be primarily motivated by Tolkien's disappointment with other works of literature, there is also narrative evidence that the ents are not quite as altruistic as they are often depicted.

Throughout Tolkien's work, much is made of the fact that Fangorn forest is now all that remains of a much larger forest that some 6000 years before covered the majority of Middle-earth and it is Saruman's wanton destruction of what little is left that finally leads Treebeard to action. Treebeard is keen to point out that 'I am not altogether on anybody's *side*, because nobody is altogether on my *side*' (Tolkien, 1995, p. 461) and when he marches on Isengard, it is very much to avenge himself on Saruman for the destruction of the forest. He tells Merry and Pippin that, 'We are never roused unless it is clear to us that *our trees* and *our lives* are in great danger' (Tolkien, 1995, p. 474, my italics) and that, 'You may be able to help me. You will be helping your friends that way, too' (Tolkien, 1995, p. 463) – both of which betray a strong degree of self-interest that simply happens to align with the needs of the hobbits. This self-interest is later seen again when, against Gandalf's request, Treebeard lets Saruman go free, because he hates 'the caging of live things' and 'will not keep even such creatures as these caged beyond great need' (Tolkien, 1995, p. 958). Treebeard regards his own morals as more important than the needs of the other races of Middle-earth, a decision that proves disastrous for the hobbits as Saruman goes on to sack their homeland, epitomising 'the basic indifference of nature to even the most momentous events in the book' (Kraus, 2004, p. 161).

While the ents are certainly not the outright villains that Tolkien first envisioned, there is certainly a strong sense of self-interest in their actions that is often overlooked. Tolkien's trees have memories, long memories, and the violent and selfish actions of Old Man Willow and the ents can be seen to be driven and justified by the hurt inflicted upon the forests by the free peoples of Middle-earth. In his essay, *'Green Time: Environmental Themes in The Lord of the Rings'*, Joe Kraus wrote 'if we could take on even a little of that perspective, it would help us to acquire the humility to recognise that we are part of a story much longer and grander than ourselves' (2004, p. 161). Far from reductive allegory, Tolkien depicted his trees as aggressive, living creatures with human emotions that perhaps posed a far greater threat to our heroes and ourselves than any contrivance of man poses to them.

He used to spend a long time on a single leaf, trying to catch its shape, and its sheen, and on the glistening of dewdrops on its edges. Yet he wanted to paint a whole tree

Leaf by Niggle

While Tolkien was quite clear about the lack of allegorical content in his Middle-earth stories, he did allow the veil to fall in his semi-autobiographical story *Leaf by Niggle. Leaf by Niggle* tells the story of Niggle, an artist who works compulsively on a single painting of a tree, neglecting other duties and becoming infuriated by those who distract him from his work:

> There was a picture in particular that bothered him. It had begun with a leaf caught in the wind, and it became a tree; and the tree grew, sending out innumerable branches, and thrusting out the most fantastic roots. Strange birds came and settled on the twigs and had to be attended to. Then all round the Tree, and behind it, through the gaps in the leaves and boughs, a country began to open out; and there were glimpses of a forest marching over the land, and the mountains tipped with snow' (Tolkien, 2001, p. 94).

Leaf by Niggle contains far more overt allegorical connections to Tolkien's world view than the Middle-earth stories. *The Lord of the Rings* took Tolkien over twelve years to write and went through countless revisions; four full volumes of *The History of Middle-earth* document this vast creative odyssey. C.S. Lewis once remarked of Tolkien that he had 'only two reactions to criticism … Either he begins the whole work over again from the beginning or else takes no notice at all' (Carpenter, 2016, p. 195) and Tolkien's frequent revision and inability to finish *The Lord of the Rings* is mirrored in Niggle's attempts to finish his painting. Conversely, on the creation of *Leaf by Niggle*, written in the late 1930s alongside the creation of *The Lord of the Rings*, Tolkien wrote, 'It was written down almost at a sitting, and very nearly in the form in which it now appears' (Carpenter, 2006, Letter 199). The comparative ease of composition of *Leaf by Niggle* implies that perhaps this story came from a more personal, or allegorical, place than the Middle-earth stories. In addition, despite his famous dislike for allegory in his Middle-earth stories, Tolkien all but confirmed the allegorical interpretation of *Leaf by Niggle* in a June 1957 letter when he wrote, 'it arose from my pre-occupation with The Lord of the Rings, the knowledge that it would be finished in great detail or not at all, and the fear (near certainty) that it would be "not at all"' (Carpenter, 2006, Letter 199).

It is perhaps not surprising that of all the potential subjects for Niggle to paint, Tolkien settled on a tree, given that he sometimes used trees as a metaphor for his whole creative process, once claiming that a story is written 'not out of the leaves of trees still to be observed, nor by means of botany and soil-science; but it grows like a seed in the dark out of the leaf-mould of the mind' (Carpenter, 2016, p. 171). Similarly, Tolkien wrote in 1951 of his original plans to create 'a body of more or less connected legend' (Carpenter, 2006, Letter 131) that sounded remarkably like Niggle's painting of the tree:

> I would draw some of the great tales in fullness, and leave many only placed in the scheme, and sketched. The cycles should be linked to a majestic whole, and yet leave scope for other minds and hands, wielding paint and music and drama. Absurd (Carpenter, 2006, Letter 131).

The penultimate sentence of this quote is often used as 'proof' that Tolkien would have enjoyed and supported the various adaptations of his work that have appeared since his death. However, this completely ignores the fact that he qualifies this by saying, 'It should possess the tone and quality that I desired... it should be "high", purged of the gross' (Carpenter, 2006, Letter 131) and Tolkien had *very* exacting standards. He famously condemned the synopsis of a proposed 1958 animated adaptation by saying 'The Lord of the Rings cannot be garbled like that' (Carpenter, 2006, Letter 210) and, upon reading the details of a proposed fan-made sequel, commented that 'there is no legal obstacle to this young ass publishing his sequel, if he could find any publisher, either respectable or disreputable, who would accept such tripe' (Carpenter, 2006, Letter 292).

However, whilst Tolkien's exacting standards may have made collaboration problematic, his use of 'absurd' demonstrates that he had realised that his attempts to create this vast body of work were impossible and that other 'hands' may be required to finish the work. Words such as 'draw' and 'sketch' in this passage evoke images of painting and it is hard not to imagine that this quote could also be used as a direct description of Niggle's painting of the tree. As if this were not connection enough, throughout his life Tolkien himself drew multiple versions of a tree called Amalion, which bore 'various shapes of leaves and many flowers small and large signifying poems and major legends' (Carpenter, 2006, Letter 253) and which many have suggested is meant to be a visual representation of Niggle's painting. Ultimately, Tolkien's love for trees extended into every aspect of his creative work; he filled his stories with the trees and forests he adored and imagined his entire Middle-earth legendarium as the vast tree of Amalion, a tree which, like Niggle, he feared would remain unfinished in his lifetime.

His trees began to sprout and grow, as if time was in a hurry and wished to make one year do for twenty

The Lord of the Rings

On 26 July 2014, visitors to Oxford University's Botanic Garden heard 'a series of strange creaks' (Townshend, 2014) and, shortly after, two huge branches of Tolkien's Tree came crashing to the ground. There was no discernible reason for the damage; Dr Alison Foster, then senior curator of the Botanic Garden, said, 'It's really hard to say what the cause was – It's something that just happens in old trees' (BBC, 2014). However, as a result of the damage, Tolkien's Tree was deemed unsafe and it was felled the following month.

The reaction to the loss of the tree was highly emotive, echoing Tolkien's own 'tree love' (Carpenter, 2006, Letter 199). Foster claimed that 'It's a tree like no other – it's just heart-breaking' (BBC, 2014); and that 'all of the staff are really sad, really upset ... It's our most important tree. It's a living, breathing thing. And our regular visitors have been really supportive' (Townshend, 2014). Words like 'heart-breaking' and 'supportive' evoke images of a bereavement, implying that the staff had a similarly emotional connection to Tolkien's Tree as he had to the poplar tree that he 'loved' and was 'anxious about' in his youth.

The loss of Tolkien's Tree is a surprisingly sad and affecting story and there is no doubt that, were he still alive, Tolkien would have mourned the loss of another friend. When the tree was felled, the Botanic Garden received numerous complaints about their action including 'one particular person [who] managed to find everyone's work emails [and] complained to the city council, actually alleging that we are Saruman' (Townshend, 2014). Extreme as these responses might be, it is perhaps unsurprising that Tolkien's somewhat vehement love of trees would be disseminated among his fans and he would no doubt be pleased to hear of their emotional connection to a tree with which he was well associated. Given that Tolkien died over forty years before the tree fell, it would be beyond a stretch to try to make a connection between the loss of the tree and the loss of the author; however, for an author who loved trees and who used the painting of a tree to summarise his entire creative output, it is hard not to feel that in some small way the loss of Tolkien's Tree represents a further loss of Tolkien himself.

Perhaps worried about such emotional reactions, the Botanic Garden were keen to reassure readers that they 'intended to propagate from the black pine' (BBC, 2014) to ensure that Tolkien's Tree could live on 'for other minds and hands' in the same way his work did. In August 2014, having received cuttings from the fallen tree, Helen Tate of Lime Cross Nursery wrote that they would 'do all that we can to successfully propagate a new clone … [and that they] have also sent some material to Derek Spicer at Kilworth Conifers, to increase the chance of success … of course, we will keep you posted on our progress' (Tate, 2014). Despite the promise to document their progress, there have been no further updates since then and, when contacted, both Tate and Spicer confirmed that the attempts to propagate the pine had failed, primarily due to the time of year being ill-suited to propagation – unfortunately meaning that my hopes of the chapter ending with news of a new Tolkien Tree sprouting for a new generation were sadly in vain.

However, whilst the attempts to create a clone of the tree may have failed, some parts of the tree have survived. When the tree was felled in 2014, a friend of mine, knowing my love of Tolkien, took a piece of the fallen tree and framed it for me along with a copy of the photograph taken by Michael Tolkien. The cutting now lives on a shelf in my office and the 'most important tree', so beloved by both Tolkien and the staff of the botanical gardens, has been sitting alongside me throughout the writing this chapter, serving as a form of inspiration or guiding spirit. Staring at the bark now, it is easy to make out the eye or mouth of an ent or to imagine the tree being alive with a 'watchful and waiting feeling' (Tolkien, 2012, p. 172) as Tolkien so evocatively described it. While the Tolkien Tree itself might not live on, Tolkien's tree of Amalion certainly does through the legacy of his legendarium and the work written by Tolkien scholars all around the world. Who knows, perhaps even this chapter itself could humbly be considered one of its smaller leaves.

If a Ragnarök would burn all the slums and gas-works, and shabby garages, and long arc-lit suburbs, it could for me burn all the works of art – and I'd go back to trees
J.R.R. Tolkien

Bibliography

BBC (2014). 'Tolkien's tree' in Oxford to be cut down. Online at ttps://www.bbc.co.uk/news/uk-england-oxfordshire-28582199, accessed 26 March 2019.

Carpenter, H. (ed.) (2006). *The Letters of J.R.R. Tolkien*, London: HarperCollins.

Carpenter, H. (2016). *J.R.R. Tolkien: A Biography*, London: HarperCollins.

Flieger, V. (2000). 'Taking the Part of Trees: Eco-Conflict in Middle-earth' in Clark, G and Timmons, D. *J.R.R. Tolkien and His Literary Resonances: Views of Middle-earth,* London: Greenwood Press, pp. 147–58.

Grimm, J. & W. (2006). *The Complete Grimm's Fairy Tales.* New York: Pantheon Books Inc.

Greenblatt, S, Cohen, W, Howard, J. E. & Eisaman Maus, K. (1997). *The Norton Shakespeare: Based on the Oxford Edition*, New York: Norton

Hammond, W.G & Scull, C. (2005). *The Lord of the Rings: A Reader's Companion*, London: HarperCollins.

Jackson, P (2002). *The Lord of the Rings: The Two Towers.* USA, New Line Cinema, Wingnut Films.

Jackson, P (2001). *The Lord of the Rings: The Fellowship of the Ring.* USA, New Line Cinema, Wingnut Films.

Jackson, P (2013). *The Hobbit: The Desolation of Smaug.* USA, New Line Cinema, Metro-Goldwyn-Mayer, Wingnut Films.

Kraus, J. (2004). 'Tolkien, Modernism, and the Importance of Tradition', in Bassham, G and Bronson, E. *The Lord of the Rings and Philosophy: One Book to Rule Them All*, Peru, Illinois: Open Court Publishing Company.

McIlwaine, C. (2018). *Tolkien: Maker of Middle-earth*, Oxford: Bodleian Library.

Tate, H. (2014). Propagating Tolkien's Black Pine. https://www.limecross.co.uk/propagating-tolkiens-black-pine/, accessed 26 March 2019.

Tolkien, C. (2002a). *J.R.R. Tolkien, The Return of the Shadow,* London: HarperCollins.

Tolkien, C. (2002b). *J.R.R. Tolkien, The Treason of Isengard,* London: HarperCollins.

Tolkien, J.R.R. (1995). *The Lord of the Rings,* London: HarperCollins.

Tolkien, J.R.R. (2001). *Tree and Leaf,* London: HarperCollins.

Tolkien, J.R.R. (2002). *The Silmarillion,* London: HarperCollins.

Tolkien, J.R.R. (2012). *The Hobbit,* London: HarperCollins.

Tolkien, J.R.R. (2017). *Beren and Lúthien.* London: HarperCollins.

Townshend, E. (2014). Tolkien's black pine: why do we love old trees? https://www.independent.co.uk/property/gardening/tolkiens-black-pine-why-do-we-love-old-trees-9650390.html, accessed 26 March 2019.

The Editors and Contributors

The Authors

Richard Mills is a Senior Lecturer at St Mary's University, London. He has been programme director for the Film and Popular Culture, Cultural Studies and Irish Studies degrees. He has published extensively on popular music, Irish literature and culture, film, fashion and British television. Richard is co-editor of *Mad Dogs and Englishness: Popular Music and English Identities* (Bloomsbury: 2017) and author of *The Beatles and Fandom: Sex, Death and Progressive Nostalgia* (Bloomsbury: 2019).

Elizabeth Parker is author of the forthcoming monograph *The Forest and the EcoGothic: The Deep Dark Woods in the Popular Imagination* and founding editor of the journal *Gothic Nature: New Directions in Eco-horror and the EcoGothic*. She is also co-editor of the collection *Landscapes of Liminality: Between Space and Place* and Television Editor of *The Irish Journal of Gothic and Horror Studies*. She currently lectures in English Literature at the University of West London.

András Fodor is a PhD student at the University of Szeged, Faculty of Arts, Doctoral School of Literature in Hungary. He has been publishing reviews and short stories since 2010 mainly in his native tongue, Hungarian. In 2016 he has won the JAKKendö-award for his manuscript of first collection of short stories, *A mosolygó zsonglör* (*The smiling juggler*), which has been published later in the same year. His research interests include spatiality, New Weird and China Miéville.

Benjamin Dalton iis a PhD candidate in French at King's College London. His work explores the interdisciplinary concept of 'plasticity' in the work of the contemporary French philosopher Catherine Malabou through putting Malabou in dialogue with narratives of bodily and neural transformation in contemporary French literature and film. Benjamin has published an interview with Malabou in *Paragraph* (Vol. 42, No. 2, 2019, pp. 238–254), and has a forthcoming article on plasticity in the novels of Marie Darrieussecq in *Dalhousie French Studies*. Benjamin also developed and led the interdisciplinary project 'Narrating Plasticity: Stories of Transformation between the Plastic Arts and Neurosciences', funded by King's College London's Culture team.

Alexander Sergeant is a Lecturer in Film and Media Theory at Bournemouth University. His research examines the historical and theoretical depths of popular fantasy filmmaking, a subject he has published on widely in a range of academic journals and edited collection. He is the co-editor of *Fantasy/Animation: Connections Between Media, Mediums and Genres* (Routledge, 2018), which was recently shortlisted for the BAFTSS award for Best Collection. He is the co-founder of *fantasy-animation.org*, a website dedicated to the exploring the relationship between fantasy cinema and the medium of animation through weekly blog posts by academics, writers, animators, fans and critics.

Bradford Lee Eden is an independent scholar and librarian. He has Master's and Ph.D. degrees in musicology, as well as an MS in library science. His recent books include *Middle-earth Minstrel: Essays on Music in Tolkien* (McFarland, 2010); *The Associate University Librarian Handbook: A Resource Guide* (Scarecrow Press, 2012); *Leadership in Academic Libraries: Connecting Theory to Practice* (Scarecrow Press, 2014), *The Hobbit and Tolkien's Mythology: Essays on Revisions and Influences* (McFarland, 2014), and the ten-volume series *Creating the 21ˢᵗ-Century Academic Library* (Rowman & Littlefield, 2015–17). He is also editor of the *Journal of Tolkien Research*, an online peer-reviewed journal available at http://scholar.valpo.edu/journaloftolkienresearch.

Leticia Cortina Aracil is an independent researcher currently working as a cicerone and cultural mediator at the city of Madrid. Her research interests include the existential interpretation of material culture with an emphasis on corporeality and its impact on the building of worldviews. She has previously worked as a lecturer at the Universidad Francisco de Vitoria and has published work on philosophical anthropology, mythology and folklore.

Damian O'Byrne is Programme Director for Production and Design at St Mary's University, Twickenham. His background is in graphic design and he teaches across a range of practical modules that focus on magazine design, digital art and photographic manipulation. His research interests have traditionally concerned digital media and specifically the role and impact of live television news from a Baudrillarian perspective. He also edits, designs and publishes *SBG* magazine, an independent magazine about wargaming in J.R.R. Tolkien's Middle-earth. Damian has recently begun to combine his personal passion for Tolkien with his academic career and is embarking on a PhD focussing on the practices of Middle-earth fan communities.

The Editors

Jon Hackett is programme director in film and communications at St Mary's University. His research interests include film and cultural theory, film history and popular music. He is currently working on a monograph with Dr Mark Duffett of Chester University on popular music and monstrosity, to be entitled, inevitably, *Scary Monsters*.

Sean J. Harrington is a lecturer in film and screen media at University College Dublin. His research interests include Lacanian psychoanalysis, animation and popular culture. He has previously published work on animation, Disney and the work of H.P. Lovecraft, and is author of *The Disney Fetish* (2015).

Index

CPSIA information can be obtained
at www.ICGtesting.com
Printed in the USA
BVHW052147141119
563857BV00018B/311/P